London, July 98

New World of Wine

New World of Wine

Max Allen
Tim Atkin
Michael Cooper
Richard Neill
John Platter
Brian St. Pierre

MITCHELL BEAZLEY

NEW WORLD OF WINE

First published in Great Britain in 1997 by Mitchell Beazley, an imprint of Reed International Books Limited, Michelin House, 81 Fulham Road, London SW3 6RB and Auckland and Melbourne

A CIP catalogue record for this book is available from the British Library

ISBN 1 85732 520 6

Commissioning Editor: Sue Jamieson
Executive Art Editor: Fiona Knowles
Panoramic photographs: Hendrick Holler/ Root Stock
Cartography: Hardlines
Production: Rachel Lynch
Additional text: Susy Atkins, Marguerite Thomas
Picture Research: Claire Gouldstone
Index: Pamela Le Gassick

Typeset in ITC Usherwood and Helvetica Neue Extended
Printed and bound in China

Contents

Authors

Max Allen

Max Allen is one of Australia's most exciting new wine writers, and has just completed his first book on wine, *Red and White*. Originally from the UK, where he worked for a wine importer, he moved to Australia several years ago and since then has established himself as one of Australia's freshest wine writers, teachers and consultants. He contributes regularly to the *Age, Epicure, Divine* and *Hotel* magazines in Australia and to *Wine* magazine in the UK.

Tim Atkin

Tim Atkin is the wine columnist for *The Observer* newspaper, with a string of awards for his wine writing, including the Glenfiddich Drinks Writer award (1988, 1990, 1993) and the UK Wine Guild's Wine Correspondent award (1991, 1992, 1994, 1996). He also contributes to *Wine, Saveur* and *Harpers* and has written two books on wine: *Chardonnay* and *Vin de Pays d'Oc*. He travels extensively for his research and has followed the rise of New World wine with particular interest. Here he has contributed the introductory sections, and those on Argentina and the rest of South America.

Michael Cooper

Michael Cooper is New Zealand's most acclaimed wine writer and has written several books on the subject including *The Wines and Vineyards of New Zealand*, and *Michael Cooper's Buyer's Guide to New Zealand Wines*. He is the wine columnist for *North and South* and *Liquor Link* magazines and the New Zealand editor of the Australian *Winestate* magazine.

John Platter

John Platter is acknowledged as South Africa's leading wine authority and is the author of the internationally respected *South African Wine Guide,* a comprehensive guide to the wine, winemakers and winelands of South Africa, now in its 18th annual edition. In addition to researching and writing this annually, he grows and makes Chardonnay on his own vineyard near Stellenbosch.

Richard Neill

Richard Neill temporarily swopped wine writing in London for winemaking in Chile, working with the wine producer Santa Carolina and exploring the other South American wine regions. Now back in the UK, he is the wine correspondent for *The Daily Telegraph* and contributes regularly to *Decanter, Esquire* and the *Time Out Eating and Drinking Guide*.

Brian St. Pierre

Brian St. Pierre is a former director of the California Wine Institute, and now lives in the UK where he works as a freelance writer. He is a regular contributor to *Decanter* magazine in the UK, and the *San Francisco Chronicle* and *Gourmet* magazine in the US, and is the author of several books on wine and food including *A Perfect Glass of Wine*.

Other contributors

Mitchell Beazley would like to thank wine writers Marguerite Thomas and Susy Atkins who contributed the New York State and Canada sections respectively.

△ *The Henschke vineyard in the Barossa Valley of South Australia has been producing excellent Shiraz for over 125 years.*

Introduction

What do a Spanish conquistador, the Dutch East India Company, the British First Fleet, a missionary and a railway have in common? The answer is that they all played a part in establishing the vineyards of the New World. Hernán Cortés planted vines in Mexico in 1522; Dutch colonists introduced them to the Cape in 1655; Captain Arthur Phillip, the first governor of New South Wales and a keen amateur gardener, tried his luck with a few cuttings at Sydney Cove in 1788; Samuel Marsden brought vines and a prayer book from Australia to New Zealand in 1819; and the completion of the railway line from Buenos Aires to Mendoza in 1885 transformed the production of Argentine wines.

The link between convict ships and a bottle of Hunter Valley Chardonnay might seem slight, but the New World's present is securely tethered to its past. Though we think of the New World as a place brimming with fashionable modern ideas, its vineyards have been around for a long time. Areas such as Constantia in South Africa and Baja California in Mexico have venerable winemaking traditions. Similarly, País in Chile, Criolla in Argentina and Mission in California are all descended from a grape variety first imported by the conquistadors.

Nevertheless, compared to the Old World winemaking countries of Europe, the Middle East and the Mediterranean, where grape varieties have been cultivated since antiquity, Australia, New Zealand, South Africa and North and South America are viticultural parvenus. In vinous terms, all these countries bear the badge of European origin, although each of them has developed inimitable specialities of its own.

It was a combination of conquest, migration and exploration which carried European vines from the harbours of Portsmouth, Amsterdam and Seville to the countries of the New World. Sooner or later, they were all colonised by vine-bearing European settlers. Most of these countries are situated in the Southern Hemisphere. The exception is North America, where many winemakers feel a closer affinity with

France and Italy than they do with Australia or South Africa. 'Beaune in the USA', the tongue-in-cheek slogan adopted by the Napa Valley's Saintsbury winery, has a semi-serious side, too.

Ironically, it was California which launched the modern New World boom. When Robert Mondavi set up his attractive Napa Valley winery in 1966, complete with a public tasting room and a Spanish, colonial-style courtyard, it was the first building of its kind since the gloomy days of Prohibition. There had been other New World pioneers – at Penfolds in Australia, Max Schubert had been making Grange Hermitage, albeit in the face of considerable criticism, since the early 1950s; and at Beaulieu in the Napa Valley, André Tchelistcheff had produced some wonderful Cabernet Sauvignons – but Mondavi's new venture was crucial to the self-esteem of New World wines. The success of his first Cabernet Sauvignon, followed by the invention of a new style of barrel-fermented Sauvignon Blanc, called Fumé Blanc, set new standards for California.

Mondavi's lead was followed by other winemakers, such as Ric Forman at Sterling, Warren Winiarski at Stag's Leap, Mike Grgich at Château Montelena, Dick Graff at Chalone, Paul Draper at Ridge, Joe Heitz at Heitz Wine Cellars and expatriate Frenchman, Bernard Portet, at Clos du Val. California began to raise its sights. Instead of apologising for the origin of their wines, the new breed of Californian winemakers were actively proud of it.

Such pride was fully justified in May 1976, when a blind tasting organised in Paris by Englishman Steven Spurrier pitted a group of California wines against some of the finest wines of Bordeaux and Burgundy. To their severe consternation, the largely French judging panel picked a Californian Chardonnay from Château Montelena and a Stag's Leap Cabernet as the best wines on the table. *Time Magazine* called it 'The Judgement of Paris'. All of a sudden, it seemed, the New World had nothing to feel inferior about.

Australia was next to take up the challenge. Until the early 1970s, the land of 'barbies' and assorted marsupials produced more fortified wines than table wines,

△ *Bright yellow mustard adds a dramatic splash of colour in the Beckstoffer Vineyard, Oakville, Napa.*

and drank more beer than both put together. But as the decade wore on, Australia began to redefine New World wine styles. Bigger, fruitier and more obvious than many Californian wines, the new breed of Australian wine was designed with a mass audience in mind and took a perverse pride in ignoring French role models. Australia grabbed hold of the kind of wines California was producing and exaggerated them: more oak, more alcohol, more intensity of flavour.

As in California, only two things mattered: the name of the producer and the name of the grape variety. So-called varietals (ie wines produced from and named by the grape variety used) simplified the complicated business of choosing and ordering wine. Australian Chardonnay, in particular, came to exemplify the modern New World wine – easy to pronounce, easy on the wallet and easy on the palate. When you bear in mind that there was no Chardonnay in South Australia, the country's most important winemaking state, until David Wynn of Mountadam planted it in 1972, you can see how rapidly the Australian wine industry has developed.

Australia has moved on since then. Its Chardonnays are subtler and the development of cool climate regions such as Coonawarra, the Adelaide Hills and the Yarra Valley has enabled it to produce a much greater range of wines than in the past. It has also rediscovered its indigenous wine styles: Barossa Valley Shiraz, Hunter Valley Sémillon and the wonderful fortified wines of Rutherglen.

But adaptability and the desire to make consumer-friendly wines continue to characterise the Australian approach. The emphasis is on producing enjoyable, flavour-charged wines. Belatedly, California has begun to adopt a similar approach. After a flirtation with tough, tannic reds in the Bordeaux style designed for long cellaring, California has moved towards the fruit-dominated New World camp in recent years. The wines of Ridge, which taste good at any stage of their development, the increasingly impressive Pinot Noirs made by the likes of Au Bon Climat, Acacia and Rochioli, and the numerous, inventive bottlings from the Bonny Doon winery are good examples of the trend.

Other New World countries have learned from the examples of Australia and

California. New Zealand has developed a world-wide following for one highly individual style of wine: its pungently grassy Marlborough Sauvignon Blancs, compared to a 'bungee jump into a gooseberry bush' by one local wine writer. Thanks to the brilliant marketing and labelling used initially by Cloudy Bay, Kiwi Sauvignon Blancs have redefined the flavour of the Loire's most famous grape. Once again, an Old World style has been exaggerated to brilliant effect. The combination of grape variety and producer has proved irresistible. This is not to say that New Zealand is a one grape country. The land of the thin white cloud is fast becoming one of the best New World producers for Pinot Noir, Chardonnay and sparkling wines.

Chile, South Africa and Argentina are not yet as successful as California and Australia, although all three of them make far more wine than New Zealand. Until recently, Chile and Argentina were happy to produce dull, old-fashioned wines for domestic palates, although a decline in local consumption has forced a rethink. And South Africa's political situation, and its reliance on over-centralisation, hampered change until the early 1990s.

But there are encouraging signs in all three countries. Chile has started to emerge as a source of elegant, crisply defined whites and fine-grained Merlots, Argentina is set to combine the best varieties of France, Italy and Spain in a new assault on the world wine market. And South Africa is slowly pulling away from the apartheid era to create a serious challenge to Australia's predominant position, with Pinotage as its strongest weapon.

What do these countries have in common? It is not immediately obvious why a New Zealand Sauvignon Blanc, an Argentine Malbec, a Chilean Chardonnay, a Californian Zinfandel, an Australian Shiraz and a South African Chenin Blanc should belong in the same New World pigeon hole. The task is further complicated by the fact that many producers have started to make blended wines, combining two or more grape varieties in apparent contradiction of the notion that 'simple is best'. But all these wines are distinguished by two things: flavour and accessibility. This, more than anything, is what defines the New World style.

△ *Steeply terraced vineyards overlooked by Paarl ('Pearl') Mountain, South Africa.*

Modern Winemaking

▽ *Gleaming stainless steel fermenting tanks at the Vergelegen winery in South Africa; founded in 1700 yet totally up-to-date.*

The Vineyard

'*Soil is dirt*,' an iconoclastic New World winemaker once famously remarked. The comment was designed to raise eyebrows and hackles in the Old World, where individual vineyard sites and their interaction with certain grape varieties are regarded with reverence. And it succeeded.

The ensuing debate illustrated the contrasting approaches which still existed back in the mid-1980s. Broadly speaking, New World wines were fashioned in the winery. As long as your vineyard was well-drained and got enough sunshine, ran the argument, you could plant almost any grape variety you chose. Technology would carry all before it. This idea was anathema to Old World winemakers, who felt that a wine should reflect its origins – what the French call its 'terroir' – not the hand of the winemaker. Both positions were over-simplified for effect. There were New World winemakers who believed in what Brian Croser of Petaluma in Australia has termed 'privileged vineyard sites', just as there were Old World winemakers who were happy to plant vines more or less anywhere. But the distinction was still valid.

Nowadays, the Old and New World positions are remarkably similar. It is widely accepted that good wines are made from good grapes and that no amount of technological tinkering can make up for basic lack of flavour. As Paul Draper of Ridge Vineyards in California puts it: 'There are certain vineyards which make themselves.' If New World cellar techniques have had an enormous impact in the Old World, then the opposite is true in the vineyard.

The New World is not as rigidly defined as the Old. Winemakers are still free to plant the grape, or grapes, of their choice. (This partly explains the appeal of the New World for winemakers from France and Italy). But increasingly, they have come to accept that certain varieties have an affinity with certain regions, be it Shiraz in the Barossa Valley, Chardonnay in Casablanca, Pinotage in Stellenbosch, Cabernet Sauvignon in the Napa Valley or Sauvignon Blanc in Marlborough.

Many of the best wineries now subscribe to the European view that great wines can only be made from low yielding vineyards sited on poor soils. In some cases, New World winemakers are literally taking to the hills. This trend has coincided with the realisation in California that AXR1, the rootstock which was widely used in the 1970s and early 1980s because of its high yields, is not resistant to the vine louse phylloxera. Nature has bitten back.

Differences remain between the Old and New Worlds, however. New World vineyards tend to be more highly mechanised, for a start. The essential tasks of pruning and harvesting are often carried out by machines, especially in vineyards where restricting costs is an important factor. European vineyards tend to be older and harder to farm – imagine a mechanical harvester struggling up the steep slopes of the Mosel or Rhône Valleys – so mechanisation is comparatively rare (and occasionally illegal) in many of the Old World's more traditional regions.

In the classic areas of the Old World, vineyard owners still place their faith in human pickers and pruners as a rule, arguing that such a job cannot be left to undiscriminating machines. Some New World producers disagree: the new generation of machines, they contend, are perfectly capable of telling ripe from unripe grapes or of pruning a vineyard satisfactorily. Others, however, are opposed to mechanical pruning, particularly where fine wines are concerned.

Mechanisation helps to explain the lay-out of many New World vineyards. At two metres by four metres, the distance between vines, and between rows of vines, is generally wider than in the Old World, where one metre by one metre is the norm. Nevertheless, there is a certain degree of cross-fertilisation here.

Some New World winemakers believe that European-style high density planting improves wine quality, while in the Old World, new vineyards are often planted with mechanisation in mind. This is especially true of modern vineyards in the Languedoc-Roussillon, the source of ten per cent of all the world's wine. The varieties grown in the New World are, almost without exception, European in origin. By a process of natural selection, the New World has chosen the grapes

△ Left: Pinotage, a Pinot Noir/Cinsaut cross. Centre: New World vineyards tend to be widely-spaced to allow for mechanisation. Right: the Australian grape harvest on a grand scale.

which adapt, and it must be said sell, best of all. The wealth of different grapes found in Italy, Spain and France is greatly reduced in the New World, although Australia and especially California do adopt new and fashionable varieties from time to time.

The New World also lacks the clonal diversity of the Old, where the best vineyards have developed and mutated over a period of centuries. In some places, such as Oregon (for Chardonnay), Australia (for Pinot Noir) and South Africa (for Chardonnay, Cabernet Sauvignon and almost everything else), planting an inappropriate clone has proved a massive three paracetamol-style headache. In others, such as New Zealand, where the Sauvignon Blanc clone imported by the Kiwis was a hit from the start, the roulette wheel produced the right result.

New World vineyards tend to be located in warmer climates, even if there has been a move in the last decade towards 'cool climate viticulture', that is planting vines in areas where weather conditions broadly resemble those of regions such as Burgundy and Bordeaux. A small but growing cool climate fan club exists in Australia, California, Chile, South Africa and especially New Zealand.

All the same, the majority of New World vineyards are planted in hot climates like California's Central Valley, Australia's Riverland and Argentina's Mendoza, all sources of sound glugging wines. Irrigation is a necessity here if the vines are to survive. The high temperatures explain why many New World wineries harvest at night or in the early morning. It is simply too hot, both for the grapes and the vineyard workers, to pick during the day.

Cool climate viticulture is highly important in at least one respect. It was the New World's chillier regions, such as Oregon and parts of New Zealand, which prompted viticulturists to look at new trellising systems and the related area of grapevine 'canopy management' (the positioning and ratio of shoots to bunches of grapes). Humidity and a comparative lack of sunshine were a perennial problem here. To reduce their harmful effects, the Australian Dr Richard Smart developed something known as 'winemaking in the vineyard'.

Smart's pioneering, if controversial, work has made him the New World's leading viticulturist, with consultancies in several different countries and the air miles to prove it. The gist of his theory is that it is access to sunlight, rather than low vineyard yields, which determines wine quality. Over-vigorous canopies with too many leaves prevent the sunlight getting through. This can lead to red wines which taste green and herbaceous with insufficient fruit ripeness, something which is still too often the case in New Zealand.

Smart's solution is to open or 'split' the canopy and to remove unnecessary leaves around the bunches. This increases 'photosynthesis', the process by which the grapes acquire sugars and without which there would be no alcohol, and therefore no wine. It also makes mechanisation more effective and, according to Smart and his disciples, can lead to higher yields with no apparent loss of wine quality.

The names of the trellising systems used, if not necessarily invented, by Smart are a mixture of the evocative (Geneva Double Curtain and the Lyre) and the practical-sounding (Scott Henry, Sylvoz and Te Kauwhata Two Tier).

Despite their cool climate origins, these systems have been adopted by some winemakers in warmer New World regions, too. In the traditional areas of the Old World, where vines tend to be trained lower to the ground, using the cane pruned, Guyot system or left as bush vines, they are seldom used. Nevertheless, 'experimental' plantings do exist and the Lyre system, developed by the Bordeaux-based academic Dr Alain Carbonneau, has begun to develop a following among producers of supposedly inferior *vins de pays*.

It could be argued that such systems are unnecessary in countries like Italy, France and Spain. The point of improved trellising in the New World is to reproduce the type of grapes which grow naturally in classic areas, with an appropriate balance between ripeness, sugar and acidity. Whatever their effectiveness in the New World, they should not be seen as a panacea for poorly sited vineyards, according to Vanya Cullen, of Cullen Wines in Australia. 'I still think climate and soil are more important than trellising,' she says. Whatever happened to 'soil is dirt'?

△ *Left: Early season in cool climate Central Otago, New Zealand. Centre: Irrigation is essential in the hot vineyards of Mendoza. Right: Gnarled Shiraz vines in South Australia's Clare Valley.*

The Winery

New World wineries are often portrayed as temples of high-tech, stuffed to the rafters with stainless steel tanks, must chillers, roto-fermenters and other bits of sophisticated winemaking kit. The reality is slightly different. While it may true that you are more likely to come across huge stainless steel 'tank farms' in Stellenbosch or the Barossa Valley than you are in Burgundy or the Mosel, traditional, some might say old-fashioned, winemaking methods are as likely to be found these days in the New World as the Old.

Once you start to look for them, the examples are surprisingly prevalent: the Californian Pinot Noir producer who climbs into the vats and treads his own grapes; the Kiwi bio-dynamic enthusiast who bottles his wines by the phases of the moon; the Australian Shiraz nut who still uses a rickety turn of the century basket press, cranking its engine like a temperamental vintage car.

Even in bigger wineries, the New World does not have exclusive access to modern technology. Many of the best European set-ups are just as up-to-date as their cutting-edge counterparts in Australia, California, Chile and South Africa. You only have to visit a top Bordeaux château or one of the better Chianti estates to see the evidence for yourself. Some of them even run to marble-floored bottling lines.

And yet it is still possible to contrast New and Old World winemaking techniques in general terms. Old World winemakers, as a rule, intervene less in the winery, believing that wine is an expression of nature's gifts and should not show the producer's thumbprints. They are also more likely to accept received wisdom as fact. 'I make wine the way my grandfather did,' is still a common refrain in many European cellars. In the New World, there is generally far less respect for the work of previous generations.

New World winemakers are constantly experimenting with new-fangled techniques, whether it be the addition of enzymes, the introduction of a special

fermentation yeast, or the use of oak 'chips', known euphemistically as micro-barrels in parts of Australia. On occasion, the pace of change can seem bewildering, with ideas discarded the moment they become unfashionable. This is especially true of California. But the New World's desire to question everything is also one of its greatest assets. Its approach is frequently more rigorous – more scientific for want of a better word – than that of the Old.

New World winemakers are usually better-trained, thanks to the demanding academic degrees offered by places such as Roseworthy in Australia and the University of California, Davis. The Geisenheim Institute in Germany and the Universities of Bordeaux and Montpellier perform the same function in Europe, of course, but a New World winemaker is more likely to hold a professional qualification. This does not necessarily produce better wines. As one well-known Californian once argued: 'You spend your first two years as a winemaker forgetting all the things you learnt as a student'. Traditional, empirical practices aren't all bad.

The application of science is what distinguishes most New World winemaking. In part, this is a response to the climate in which the wines are produced. New World regions tend to be hotter than the classic regions of Europe, so high standards of hygiene, and the use of 'cultured' instead of 'wild' yeasts, must chillers and temperature-controlled fermentations are arguably more important because of the enhanced risk of bacterial spoilage.

New World wines are generally produced in shiningly clean environments, although cellars in parts of Argentina can still be rather rustic. Hoses and a bottomless supply of clean water are vital for washing down tanks, barrels and winery floors. You could almost eat your lunch straight off the tiles – not something you'd want to do in, say, the majority of Portuguese, Spanish or French cooperatives.

This explains the success of so-called flying winemakers over the last decade. These evocatively-named oenologists are (usually) young Southern Hemisphere winemakers who come to Europe for a few weeks during the Northern Hemisphere's vintage. They jet, drive or walk in, make the wine and leave, as a rule, even if many

△ Left: Grapes tumble into the crusher at Lindemans, Victoria. Right: Stainless steel and wood co-exist in the cellars of the La Agricola cooperative, Mendoza.

of them come back again the following year. Their appeal is simple. Applying New World standards of hygiene to old-fashioned wineries starved of finance and creative energy can produce dramatic results in places like Hungary, Bulgaria, Spain, Italy and France, yielding clean wines with attractive fruit flavours for everyday drinking.

The increasing importance of flying winemakers (see page 20) shows how much the Old World still has to learn from the New, although there are signs that local European winemakers in less favoured regions are beginning to catch on to the range of tricks and procedures used by the airborne division. (Akos Kamocsay in Hungary is a good example.)

How do they do it? Cleanliness is part of the answer. But so is the exclusion of oxygen, which is generally harmful to wines, especially white wines. Old World winemakers are less worried about protecting their wines, which partly explains the greater incidence of 'oxidised' wines in traditional regions. Their New World counterparts can be obsessive about it – pressing the grapes with care and blanketing the wines with inert gases to keep oxygen away. This can produce faultless wines which are almost too clean for their own good, but most people would rather taste a fresh white than a stale one.

Another commonly-used technique is temperature-controlled fermentation, usually in stainless steel tanks, to retain freshness and fruity flavours in the finished wines. In this respect, Old World producers were held back by lack of investment in the past. A lot of traditional cooperatives are still dramatically short of cash. Using modern technology is arguably easier than paying to install it.

The New World relies on cultured, pure yeasts for its fermentations to a far greater degree than the Old. Once again, the emphasis is on controlling what goes on in the winery and minimising the risk of off flavours. In the Old World, producers often allow the wines to ferment naturally, permitting the wild yeasts found on the grapeskins to take their course.

It hasn't all been a one way process, however. The cellars of the Old World have influenced the New, too, especially when it comes to the Burgundian grapes, Pinot

Noir and Chardonnay. Some New World producers are moving away from reductive techniques and exposing their wines to a limited amount of oxygen in a search for greater complexity. Other Old World techniques which are used in the New include punching or treading down the 'cap' of grapeskins and pips during fermentation, and the stirring of fermentation lees in barrel, known as bâttonage in France, to add richness to white wines. The growing incidence of 'unfiltered' wines is part of the same trend.

New World wines tend to be oakier in flavour than those from the Old, as producers use a greater proportion of new oak and are more likely to use less subtle American oak than French, especially for red wines. On occasion New World producers finish fermenting their reds in barrel, something which is rare in the Old World. And for cheaper wines, winemakers are not frightened to use 'chips' to impart some toasty oak flavours in the short-term. Chips are illegal in many European regions.

Levels of alcohol are often higher in the New World and winemakers frequently leave a little natural sweetness in their wines. Both things provide what winemakers call 'mouthfeel', making them approachable and easy to drink in their youth – a quality which is sometimes regarded with suspicion in parts of Europe. There is also a greater incidence of acid-adjustment in the New World. The Old World commonly, and just as legitimately, relies on added sugar to increase alcohol – a process known as chaptalisation. Both additions are used to produce better balanced wines.

Despite the widespread use of oak, the majority of New World wines remain what Australians call 'fruit-driven', with the emphasis on primary flavours and the inherent character of the grape variety, or varieties. Outside the cooler, more marginal areas, wines are pretty consistent from one year to the next. As a rule, blended wines are fuller-flavoured, and tend to be made to a formula in the winery.

Reliability is central to the New World's appeal; it has helped encourage sales of these wines worldwide. In North America, and in the vineyards of the Southern Hemisphere, winemakers are expected to provide it.

△ *New oak barriques line the immaculate Opus One winery in Napa Valley, co-founded by Baron Philippe de Rothschild and Robert Mondavi.*

The Winemakers

Winemakers are the film stars of the booze business. Their names appear on labels, their photographs appear in advertisements and their opinions are quoted with reverence in the media. This is a comparatively recent trend. Thirty years ago, the identity of the person who made a particular wine was unimportant. Domaines in parts of France, especially Burgundy, might have been named after their owners, but no one showed any great interest in meeting them, let alone inviting them to give a press conference or tutor a tasting for 200 consumers.

How things have changed. Thanks to the New World, winemakers are much more prominent these days. There are a few internationally-recognised names in the Old World – Miguel Torres in Spain, Paul Pontallier and Michel Rolland in Bordeaux, Dominique Lafon in Burgundy, Gérard Chave in the Rhône or flying winemakers such as Frenchman Jacques Lurton, Portuguese-based Australian, Peter Bright, Master of Wine Kym Milne and Englishman, Hugh Ryman – but the cult of the winemaker is essentially a New World phenomenon.

It is significant that many of the best-known Old World producers also make wine in California or the Southern Hemisphere. Torres, Pontallier and Rolland can all be found in Chile at various times during the year. Christian Moueix of Château Pétrus has his own estate in California, Dominus, following the lead of the late Philippe de Rothschild, who set up a joint venture with the Napa Valley's Robert Mondavi, called Opus One. And the leading flying winemakers are well-nigh ubiquitous. Hugh Ryman, to cite only one example, makes or has made wine in Chile, South Africa, France, Moldova, Germany, Hungary, Argentina, Spain, Corsica and Australia. The man rarely gets the chance to sleep under his own roof.

When did the apotheosis of the winemaker begin? Most commentators would agree that it really kicked off in the 1960s. There were, to be sure, famous winemakers in the New World before this time – André Tchelistcheff at Beaulieu

Vineyards in California and Max Schubert at Penfolds in Australia – but it was the establishment of the modern Californian wine industry which brought the winemaker to the fore. Men like Robert Mondavi, Warren Winiarski of Stag's Leap, Paul Draper of Ridge and Bernard Portet of Clos du Val (another Frenchman working overseas) became stars, especially once their wines started to beat the French classics in comparative tastings.

The influence of this trend was felt in other parts of the New World, most conspicuously in Australia, which was beginning to develop as a wine-producing country, switching its focus from fortified wines (so called 'stickies') to dry table wines. Characterful figures, such as Len Evans and Murray Tyrrell in the Hunter Valley, brought wine to the general Aussie drinker. Slowly, wine was replacing beer on the dinner table down under.

It was the next generation that really increased the profile and public awareness of winemaking in Australia. Big company winemakers such as John Duval of Penfolds, Philip Shaw of Rosemount, Robin Day of Orlando, Brian Walsh of Yalumba and especially the brash, bow tie-wearing Wolf Blass have become powerful figures in the new Australian industry, aided by the growing publicity surrounding the various national wine shows. If Wolf Blass didn't exist, someone would have had to have invented him.

Smaller sized companies have their stars, too. Thanks to the growing internationalisation of the wine scene, winemakers such as Adam Wynn of Mountadam, Dr Andrew Pirie of Piper's Brook, Rocky O'Callaghan of Rockford, David Hohnen of Cape Mentelle (and the grey matter behind Cloudy Bay in New Zealand) and Brian Croser of Petaluma are known all over the globe. Along with his business partner Dr Tony Jordan, Croser in particular was revered as a technical guru in the early 1980s. Several flying winemakers, including Hugh Ryman and Martin Shaw, were formed in the Petaluma cauldron.

The success and expertise of Croser and Jordan encouraged the belief that winemakers were modern-day alchemists capable of turning dull grapes into fine

Left: The Casablanca Valley, Chile, in the shadow of the Andes. Right (left to right): Flying winemakers Jacques Lurton and Kym Milne; viticulturist Dr Richard Smart; and Rosemount's Philip Shaw.

wine at the drop of a packet of cultured yeast. Things have changed since then. There is a far greater awareness of the importance of viticulture in the New World than there was 20 years ago; as a result, the all-powerful image of the winemaker has been revised somewhat. New World viticulturists such as Richard Smart, Master of Wine Steve Smith and Dr David Jordan (no relation to Tony) have become significant figures in their own right.

The profile of winemakers is still far higher than that of viticulturists, however, as evidenced by the proliferation of 'signed', winemaker labels. Many of the smaller wineries in Australia – Tim Adams, Charles Melton, Grant Burge and Tolley's, for example – are named after their owner and winemaker. This is less true in Chile, South Africa, New Zealand and even California these days, although the biggest winery in the US, and the world for that matter, is named after two wine men – Ernest and the late Julio Gallo.

Not all winemakers in the New World are male, of course. In fact there is probably a greater percentage of female winemakers in the New World than in the Old. The best-known names are Pam Dunsford of Chapel Hill and Vanya and Di Cullen at Cullen's in Australia, Zelma Long at Simi in California, Norma Ratcliffe at Warwick in South Africa and Kate Radburnd and Jenny Dobson in New Zealand.

Flying winemakers apart, the best-known New World winemakers are concentrated in California and Australia, the two leading quality wine-producing countries. The famous faces in California these days include Randall Grahm, the maverick owner of Bonny Doon, who has made his name with an ever-shifting lineup of Italian and Southern French grapes, Jim Clendenen of Au Bon Climat, Larry Brooks of Acacia and Pinot Noir specialists Dick Ward and David Graves of Saintsbury. But Robert Mondavi and Warren Winiarski are still there, too.

Other New World countries have a smaller pool of talent, with fewer wineries to go round. In places like Chile and Argentina, many of the leading lights are international consultants – the American Paul Hobbs or the Frenchman Michel Rolland, for instance – but indigenous winemaking talent is also starting to flourish.

Significantly, the foreign winemakers who come to Chile tend to be more than flying visitors. Most have long-term connections with individual wineries, giving them the opportunity to develop a consistent style. Chile has a handful of good winemakers including Ignacio Recabarren of Viña Casablanca, Alvaro Espinoza of Carmen and Andres Ilabaca of Santa Rita, as does Argentina in Jorge Riccetelli of Norton, Angel Mendoza of Trapiche and Rodolfo Montenegro of La Agricola.

South Africa's sojourn in the wilderness – the result of international and moral trade sanctions – means that its best winemakers are under-appreciated outside the Cape. But as South Africa's wines increase in popularity, so its winemakers are enjoying a higher profile. The four winemakers who have had the greatest impact are Danie de Wet, the Chardonnay king of Robertson, Charles Back of Fairview, who is South Africa's answer to Randall Grahm, Gyles Webb of Thelema and Beyers Truter, whose Kanonkop Pinotages are among the best wines coming out of South Africa. The emergence of Pinotage as the Cape's most newsworthy grape may bring other to the fore.

New Zealand also has few internationally-recognised names. Indeed, some of its most celebrated winemakers – Pinot Noir genius Larry McKenna of Martinborough, Jane Hunter of Hunter's and Kevin Judd of Cloudy Bay – are in fact Australians. However, local talent is ably represented by the likes of Master of Wine Michael Brajkovich of Kumeu River, who makes one of the New World's best Chardonnays, Tim Finn of Neudorf, Mark Robertson of Matua Valley, Kim Crawford of Coopers Creek and the Pinot Noir obsessives Neil McCallum of Dry River and Clive Paton of Ata Rangi. As in South Africa, New Zealand's growing reputation as a wine producing nation should enhance the fame of its best producers.

Are any of these New World winemakers as well-known as politicians, pop singers or super models? Of course not. It's hard to imagine a winemaker filling the Albert Hall or the Joe Louis Arena. Talent comes into it, but in the final analysis, a winemaker is only a technician. As the Old World realised a long time ago, the real stars are to be found in the vineyard, not the winery.

△ Left to right: Famed Australian winemakers James Halliday and Brian Croser; US innovators Randall Grahm and Jim Clendenen. Far right: The Casablanca Valley, Chile.

Australia

AUSTRALIA IS A VAST COUNTRY. Massive. It is the same size as the United States – not counting Alaska – but it is home to a mere 18 million people. These people are scattered around the fertile green edges of their big red land, but despite the enormous distances between them they share a sometimes remarkably strong sense of community. Australia may be a vast country, but it often feels more like a small country town.

It is not surprising then to find that this country's wine industry is one of the most unified in the world. A small, weekend hobbyist with an acre of vines on the chilly south coast of Tasmania feels just as much a part of the industry as the chief winemaker for one of the big South Australian companies with thousands of acres of vineyards stretching away into the shimmering distance. At the turn of the 21st century, the Australian wine industry is more unified and successful than ever before.

▽ *Coldstream Hills, Yarra Valley, Victoria. The natural amphitheatre makes a perfect suntrap for ripening grapes.*

It is worth having a brief look at the 200-year history of wine here in order to explain why the current good times are so welcome, and to add a little depth to the common perception of Australia as a gleaming, brand new wine country.

Captain Arthur Phillip proudly planted the first vines at what was to become Sydney in 1788, only days after the First Fleet arrived in the new colony, and people immediately started predicting big things for wine from 'Down Under'. Australia was hailed in its early years as 'John Bull's vineyard', a virtual paradise for viticulture, destined to produce fine wines for the tables of the Empire. Pioneers struck out across the land clutching vine cuttings.

By the 1870s the prediction seemed to be coming true, with Australian vineyards winning gold medals in Paris and London for their light wines, modelled loosely on the classic styles of Europe. Unfortunately, those same vineyards were to disappear a few short years later, either wiped out by the vine louse phylloxera, overtaken by

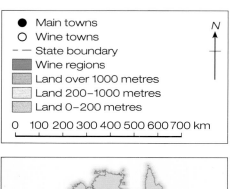

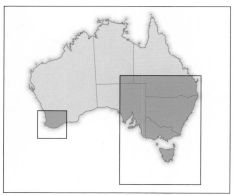

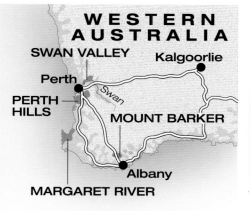

dairy farming, or simply falling redundant as the Australian national palate developed a thirst for beer and fortified wine.

By the end of the First World War, South Australia and Victoria were producing great quantities of 'port', 'sherry' and heavy red, much of which found its way to the Old Country. By the early 1930s, Australia was exporting more wine to Britain than France – mostly in bulk. But by the end of the Second World War, export demand had diminished and domestic drinkers seemed to prefer fortified wines. The future looked dismal for the quality table wines we associate with Australia today.

Then, in the 1960s, interest picked up again for table wine and the domestic boom began. But over the ensuing 20 years, the re-nascent industry over-estimated demand, and as recently as the mid-1980s, priceless old vines like Shiraz and Grenache were pulled out of the ground in a government-sponsored scheme to reduce the glut of wine. Ironically, this coincided with the beginnings of the current export boom in markets that are now clamouring for wines made from these old vines.

Today, that export boom continues to grow and the industry is buoyant. It aims to treble production by the year 2025 and become the world's most profitable wine exporter. But why is Australian wine so popular? What is the secret of its success?

Many Old World winemakers will, rather dismissively, put it all down to technology, and in one sense they are right. Australia has an enviable record of technological innovation in the chemistry of winemaking and viticultural techniques. Australian winemakers also have a remarkable magpie-like ability to understand, adapt and improve on other countries' techniques and innovations. That history of critical appreciation has also formed the backbone of Australia's famed winemaking schools. Roseworthy and Charles Sturt University at Wagga Wagga produce some of the most scientifically knowledgeable and critical winemakers in the world. But while Australia's wholehearted embrace of technology is responsible for its consistently fault-free, reliable wines, technology is not the only answer.

Most important are the vineyards. In the 1980s, winemaking techniques received all the attention. Now the emphasis is back outside. Standing among perfectly-trained, healthy, grape-laden vines, rust-red soils under your boots, wide blue skies above you, the Australian advantage is clear.

Far from coincidentally, Australia is also in the process of legally defining and registering its wine regions as a result of a 1994 trade agreement with the EU. While this simple appellation system will have little impact on the already straightforward labelling of Australian wines (another important factor in their success in export markets), it is prompting thought within the industry as to which varieties do best where, and which vineyards do better than their neighbours. In some ways, it is a tentative acknowledgment of the French idea of terroir. With the emphasis on blending, this 'foreign' concept has tended to be overlooked by winemakers thus far.

The legendary winemakers of Australia, such as Max Schubert of Penfolds, understood the importance of diversity in the choice of grape types and cultivation. It is vital that the developing Australian appellation system remains flexible and allows viticultural and winemaking freedom to continue. Because, at the end of the day, the Australian wine industry's greatest asset is its freedom.

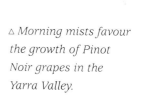

△ *Morning mists favour the growth of Pinot Noir grapes in the Yarra Valley.*

New South Wales

The large state of New South Wales is home to some of Australia's oldest wine regions, as well as some of its youngest. These regions range across the climatic spectrum, from the intense heat of the Hunter Valley two hours drive north of Sydney, to the brisk high-altitude chill of new vineyards in the Snowy Mountains in the south of the state.

Not surprisingly, wine styles also run the gamut, from sparkling to fortified, with some of Australia's best Sémillons – both crisply unwooded and lusciously botrytis-affected – standing out as highlights in the middle.

New South Wales is also a good example of the wine family tradition that runs deep in Australia's viticultural history. Some of Australia's most notable wine companies started in this state – Tyrrells and McWilliams in the last century, De Bortoli and Rosemount in this – and while they have all expanded, and now have interests across Australia, they are all still family-owned and operated. The maintenance of that tradition, in a time of increased corporate focus and aggressive company takeovers, is important.

Lower Hunter

This place defies logic. It's hot in the Hunter Valley, sometimes very hot indeed – although late afternoon thunderstorms frequently cool the place down. It also often rains when rain is least wanted: right in the middle of harvesting. These two extremes make good vintages less common than average vintages, yet the Hunter Valley has managed to produce some spectacularly good wines over the years, ensuring that the region's reputation outweighs the size of its production.

This reputation has also been considerably enhanced by some larger-than-life winemaking characters: figures such as the pioneering doctor Henry John Lindeman who did much for the region's fame in the last century, and the irrepressibly

opinionated Murray Tyrrell who has done much for it in this, both through his promotion of the area and through sometimes stunning wines.

Since the 1960s, when Max Lake (another doctor) began a revival of interest in the Hunter with his Lake's Folly vineyard, the region has become one of New South Wales' most popular tourism destinations. As one Hunter vigneron wryly observed, the Hunter may not be the easiest place in Australia to make wine, but it is the easiest place to sell it.

The region has a wide variety of soils (as do most of Australia's wine districts), but the best vineyards around Pokolbin are either on deep brown loam or red duplex. Traditional grape varieties are Sémillon and Shiraz, the former making youthfully grassy, light-alcohol unwooded white wines that can blossom into wonderfully complex, toasty wines with bottle age, the latter producing deliciously earthy, warm reds with soft, sometimes surprisingly elegant structures. Chardonnay and Cabernet appeared here in the 1960s, and produce characteristically rich, honeyed whites and chunky, earthy reds respectively.

Upper Hunter

Whereas the Lower Hunter has produced wine continuously over the last 150 years, the Upper Hunter, to the northwest, started as long ago as 1828. The first vines were planted at Dalwood, but enthusiasm soon waned; it was revived again in the 1960s in a quiet flurry of planting activity, most notably by the now-famous Rosemount winery and vineyards, still the area's largest concern, with a world-class reputation.

At first, the revival saw many vineyards planted to red grapes, but it soon became obvious that the Upper Hunter, with its heat and its well-drained dark loam soils, was better suited to white grapes.

Sémillon and Chardonnay now dominate the area. The Sémillon is picked riper and produces wines – often successfully oak-matured – with more richness than Sémillon in the Lower Hunter, while Chardonnay can, especially from Rosemount's Roxburgh vineyard, produce some of Australia's most opulent dry white wines.

△ *Machine harvesting at the Lindemans winery in the Lower Hunter Valley; rain at this moment can prove disastrous.*

Mudgee

The fertile, rich soils of Mudgee, to the west of the Lower Hunter – the famous Mudgee mud – were the initial attraction for entrepreneurial types drawn to the goldfields here in the last century. They realised the potential market in a settlement of thirsty goldminers (as did the early wine-growers at Rutherglen in northeast Victoria), and set out to make wine.

By the end of the 19th century, a thriving wine community had been established here, but by 1960, there was only one winery in the area. Then the revival of the Hunter spread to Mudgee, and the region once again is making a name for full-flavoured, warm wines.

Rich Chardonnay is the principal white wine, with Sémillon (riper and rounder than the Lower Hunter) bringing up the rear. Cabernet and Shiraz both produce big, ripe wines here that, at their best, sit plumply on the middle of the tongue.

Riverina

The dry plains around Griffith, some 300 miles west of Sydney, were brought to life in the first two decades of this century when water was diverted from the Murrumbidgee river to irrigate the land.

Vines were soon introduced on a large scale, with the combination of plentiful sun and water producing record crops in the Riverina. For 50 years wine companies such as McWilliams made an endless stream of fortified wine, but with the table wine boom of the 1960s, this region became an important source of simple red and white plonk, mostly sold as bag-in-box, or 'cask' wine.

Then, in the early 1980s, the De Bortoli wine company latched onto a different wine style equally suited to the climatic conditions of the Riverina: luscious, sweet Sémillon made from late-harvest grapes shrivelled by the noble rot, *Botrytis cinerea*. Others have followed suit, and the region is now home to a host of producers of golden 'stickies': hedonistically rich and overflowing with flavours of butterscotch, honey and apricots.

Other Areas

Sydney was the first home of the vine in Australia; as early as 1788 settlers arrived with vines for experimental planting here. The city is near the 34th parallel of latitude, making it the southern equivalent of North Africa. Consider the reputation of Moroccan wines and it becomes clear that quality winemaking here was never going to be easy – the climate is simply too warm. A couple of small vineyards, some revivals of original wineries, others brand new, are currently in operation on the fringes of the city. Unfortunately, they can suffer the same problem of excessive humidity that bedevilled the 19th-century growers, and are more of a curiosity than anything else. In these conditions wines tend to be 'flabby' with too much sugar and not enough acidity.

There are other, far more successful regions scattered around the state. The most northerly, near Port Macquarie, is home to just one winery, Cassegrain, which has defied the hot conditions to produce some good wines, both from conventional varieties such as Chardonnay, and oddities like the red grape Chambourcin.

The most southerly region is found at Tumbarumba, high up in the Snowy Mountains, just before the border with Victoria. This area is showing great promise with Chardonnay and Pinot Noir for sparkling wine.

Canalized water works miracles for the aptly-named Murrumbidgee Irrigation Area some 500 kilometres southwest of Mudgee. This area was bush country until the arrival of water and at first the intense heat here meant only heavy, fortified wines were feasible. Subsequently technology has come to the rescue with temperature-controlled fermentation tanks; cool fermentation means that not all that sugar in the grapes need turn to alcohol and also that the aroma of ripe fruit can be preserved. Today the McWilliam's winery makes excellent fresh, light wines here.

The other disparate regions, all inland, have climates best described as continental: essentially cool from being at fairly high altitude, but warmed by the bright Australian sun. That extra altitude gives them a definite quality advantage over the growers on the plains. The Canberra District was the first to be established in the early 1970s, with a handful of weekend winemakers – doctors and civil servants – pursuing their passion at boutique wineries fringing the Australian Capital Territory. Varieties such as Riesling and Chardonnay can grow well here, as can Cabernet Sauvignon in a leafy style and even Shiraz, in a taut, peppery style.

Other regions followed, all on the western slopes of the Great Dividing Range. Cowra was first; its vineyards flourish at 1,800 feet and the resulting aromatic Chardonnays are much admired. Next came what is now called the Hilltops region, near Young, and the latest addition is the Orange district wine region, perched on the side of an extinct volcano.

Each of these newer districts has produced some wonderful wines in the last 20 years, and all three have attracted the attention of well-known producers – first Rothbury and Petaluma at Cowra, then McWilliams at Barwang in the Hilltops region and finally Rosemount Estate at Orange. Chardonnay is the buzz-word in all three regions, with Shiraz and Cabernet also excelling at Hilltops, and the aromatic whites, Sauvignon Blanc and Riesling, showing glimpses of greatness at Orange.

△ *Signs of rebirth for the Mudgee region which has a favourably cool climate for Chardonnay and Cabernet Sauvignon; the Montrose vineyard is the largest in the district.*

South Australia

South Australians will tell you that they live in the most important wine state in the country, and in a way they are absolutely right. South Australia produces more wine than any other state (largely because of the huge, refinery-like wineries and endless broad-acre vineyards of the Riverland), and is home to some of the most well-established and best-known wine regions.

You see, South Australia was not as badly affected by the dark ages of wine during the early and middle years of this century as much of Victoria was. Phylloxera never took hold here as it did across the border, and the warmth of this state's established regions meant that when popular tastes changed from table to fortified wine early this century, so could South Australia's winemakers, with ease.

Coincidentally – and luckily – this continuous history means that South Australia, particularly in the Barossa and McLaren Vale, has a fairly strong gastronomic tradition. The wine and food cultures in these places have grown up together, and pre-date the current modish interest in regional food and regional wine by decades.

Much of this heritage, of course, stems from the strong influence of the non-Anglo-Celt migrants in these areas: the Germans in the Barossa and, more recently, the Italians in McLaren Vale. The migrant contribution is important elsewhere in the story of Australian wine, but nowhere is it as deliciously visible as in South Australia. Barossa ham or sausage with a big glass of Barossa Shiraz; plump McLaren Vale olives with McLaren Vale Sangiovese; these are simple food and wine combinations with decades of tradition behind them.

Adelaide and the Hills

South Australia's wine history began in what is now Adelaide suburbia and, almost miraculously, two of the most important of these first vineyard sites still exist. John Reynell's Chateau Reynella (now considered to be at the northern edge of McLaren

Vale) and Christopher and Mary Penfold's Magill Estate are both splendidly restored, standing as small patches of green among the shopping malls and petrol stations.

Today, Adelaide has two wine regions it can call its own. One consists of a few vineyards and wineries scattered across the hot, flat country to the north of the city known as the Adelaide Plains. The majority of the production here is handled by the large Barossa Valley Estate wine company but one small winemaker, Joe Grilli at Primo Estate, shines brilliantly with unusual and delicious wines that defy their climatic provenance.

Far more interesting from a quality point of view is the Adelaide Hills region to the east of the city (the Eden Valley, once considered part of the northern reaches of 'the Hills', is now more closely associated with the Barossa.

Up high in often beautiful hilly country, some of Australia's finest producers (most of them drawn here from other regions) are turning out excellent cool-climate wines. Sauvignon Blanc has found its Australian home here, with the long growing season producing piercingly aromatic, intensely-flavoured wines. Pinot Noir and Chardonnay, not surprisingly, excel either in sparkling wine (the most famous of which is Petaluma's Croser), or complex still wines. Merlot is the most promising of the fuller red varieties, making wines of rich, velvety softness.

Barossa Valley and Eden Valley

The Barossa is, after Coonawarra, South Australia's best-known region. It is home to many of the really big names in Australian wine – Penfolds and Orlando have some of their main winemaking facilities here – as well as a vocal and colourful collection of smaller producers such as St Hallett, Rockford and Peter Lehmann.

The valley was settled famously by German (or, more correctly Silesian Lutheran) migrants from the 1840s on, and this heritage is still strongly felt in the names, language, food and architecture of the area. Barossa *Deutsch* is still spoken, and many of the original churches still stand. The German connection also explains the continued local affection for the Riesling grape variety.

△ *Above left: Historic vinelands of Australia; grapes were first planted here at Seppeltsfield in the Barossa Valley as early as 1850.*
Above right: Ancient Shiraz vine.

Because of its rich continuous viticultural heritage, the Barossa has fairly clearly defined sub-regions. Winemakers will tell you, and indeed spell it out for you in the glass, that there is a subtle difference between Shiraz, for example, grown at Kalimna to the north of the valley, and Shiraz grown at Lyndoch to the south. Soils – the brown loam or grey sand that typify the region – and slight differences in climate have much to do with these stylistic nuances, but very often a site's unique flavours have more to do with vine age.

The Barossa (and McLaren Vale south of Adelaide) are blessed with some of the most ancient commercially productive vines on the planet. It is not uncommon to find gnarled old Shiraz and Grenache here that is 100 years old, producing incomparably concentrated hatfuls of wine each vintage.

Of course we hardly ever get to taste the produce of these special sites in its unadulterated form. Most Barossa wines are blends: wines that combine the individual character of each vineyard to produce something that is, hopefully, greater than the sum of its parts.

Riesling has been the dominant white variety in the Barossa Valley for the best part of the last 150 years. The valley floor is actually a little too warm for the variety, so most of the fruit for the Barossa's tastiest Riesling is now sourced from the cooler Barossa Ranges or Eden Valley to the southeast, which vies with the Clare Valley in South Australia and Great Southern in Western Australia as being the best for this aromatic white grape.

Shiraz is the best performing red variety in the Barossa, producing rich, leathery, exotically-flavoured wines although Cabernet can also be good, and Grenache and Mourvèdre sometimes impress, most often in blends. Chardonnay succeeds here as it does everywhere else, making rich, flavoursome wines, and Barossa Sémillon, utterly unlike Sémillon in the Hunter Valley, is usually combined with barrel-maturation to produce big, soft whites. It is also occasionally used to make deliciously luscious botrytis-affected wines.

Eden Valley, in the flat hills to the southeast of the Barossa past the town of Angaston,

has much the same soils as the Barossa but benefits from the slightly cooler, higher altitude. This is great white wine country. The Hill-Smiths, of Barossa family firm Yalumba, have their Pewsey Vale, Heggies and Hill-Smith vineyards here, each producing wonderful Riesling, Viognier and Sauvignon Blanc respectively.

This is also where the famous Henschke winery is situated: Eden Valley Shiraz, as gloriously exemplified by the Henschke Hill of Grace, successfully combines richness and elegance, while Eden Valley Pinot Noir and Chardonnay (notably at Mountadam vineyard) can do the same.

McLaren Vale and Langhorne Creek

McLaren Vale, an hour's drive south of Adelaide, is home to some lovely soft, round, easygoing wines. Rolling hills, olive groves, almond trees and fertile country characterise the land, which is enjoying particular success at the moment with generous, rich red wines.

Ever since the first vines were planted here in the 1830s and 1840s, the wines of McLaren Vale – mostly red or fortified – have been in demand, either bottled on their own or as useful blending material for winemakers in other regions. McLaren Vale, for instance, was a major supplier of 'burgundy' to England in the middle years of this century via the Emu Wine Company.

Hardys, one of Australia's best-known winemaking companies, has its headquarters here at historic Reynella, as do some of the country's better-known small winemakers such as D'Arenberg, Geoff Merrill and Wirra Wirra.

This region's reputation for reliable wine quality lies in the warm climate, the moderately fertile soils (varying from sand around Blewitt Springs to rich, red loam around the township of McLaren Vale itself), and the high occurrence of old, low-yielding vines, grown without irrigation. These wonderful old vines are the secret of the intense reds of McLaren Vale. Grenache, Shiraz, Mourvèdre (or Mataro as it's often called here) are much sought-after with the 1990s thirst for spicy, Rhône-style wines, and the ancient vines here produce particularly concentrated examples.

△ South of Adelaide, across the Onkaparinga river, lie the vineyards of McLaren Vale, famed for powerful 'port' and Shiraz.

Cabernet Sauvignon can also be excellent – rich and mouthcoating, but with supple tannins – while among the whites, Sauvignon Blanc easily claims the crown (in a rich, tropical fruit style), although Chardonnay and even Riesling can occasionally impress. Vintage 'port', while a dying breed, is singing its swan song here, with Australia's best coming from Hardy's and Chateau Reynella.

Langhorne Creek, to the southeast of McLaren Vale, has an equally long history but is today home to fewer wineries, although the region's vineyards have historically supplied fruit to many other South Australian wineries, the most famous being Wolf Blass and Saltram. The first vines were established by Frank Potts at Bleasdale in 1850 (the vineyard was named after the Reverend Bleasdale, the 19th century's answer to Australia's most famous wine personality, Len Evans), and the Potts family still make the region's best wines there.

The soils are fertile and deep, and the vineyards are often flood-irrigated. The climate is warm, although the proximity to the sea can offset the heat. The wines are even softer and rounder than those from McLaren Vale, and at their best the Cabernets can be the epitome of warm, rich South Australian red wine.

Clare

On paper the region of Clare doesn't look like being a great place for growing some of Australia's finest Riesling. It's warm, for a start, with summer temperatures often matching the Barossa Valley to the southwest. But it does indeed produce excellent Riesling – and some great reds – and has done for well over a century.

The town of Clare was established in the 1840s and soon became an important centre for the miners and wheat farmers intent on taking full advantage of the natural resources of the surrounding countryside. Vines were established at the outset, and many of the region's characteristically solid stone buildings were specifically constructed as wineries.

The Stanley Wine Company (now called Leasingham and owned by Hardy's) was one of two large Clare producers in the early years of this century, exporting much of its

wine to England (the other big winery being Quelltaler, now part of the Mildara Blass empire). Today the Taylors winery, known as Wakefield on labels destined for overseas markets, is the largest in the region, but it is the smaller producers such as Wendouree, Grosset and Sevenhill that give the Clare its real colour.

The region is stunningly beautiful in parts, with undulating hills and an occasional lush greenness after rain. It has distinct sub-regions, with the Polish Hill district to the east cooler (due to its altitude) than, for example, the Watervale district in the middle of the long thin valley. Soils vary from deep red to brown loam, with a fair amount of lime-rich subsoils, and the area's many hills offer a range of great sloping aspects for the vines.

Riesling from Clare – especially from Watervale and Polish Hill – is characterised by a zesty, lime juiciness and often stunning intensity of flavour. It can also age superbly with ten or more years in the bottle into profoundly complex, harmonious white wine. Occasionally, botrytis-affected Rieslings are made, their lusciousness perfectly cut by intense acidity.

Chardonnay is not as successful in Clare – not because the conditions are wrong, but more due to the producers' greater historical interest in Riesling (Sémillon often makes a better wooded white). The reds vary from relatively elegant Cabernets, either straight or blended with Merlot or Malbec, to huge, dense and powerful Shiraz or Shiraz blends.

Coonawarra

Coonawarra is probably the most talked about patch of vineyard land in Australia. Its famous terra rossa soils (thin, brick-red earth over deep limestone) are known the world over, and its Cabernets are widely considered Australia's best.

But this reputation obscures the fact that Coonawarra's position at the top of Australia's wine hierarchy is only 40 years old. It was first recognised as a potentially perfect winegrowing area in the 1890s, but its then too-great distance from either Adelaide or Melbourne (it is half-way between the two, just on the South Australian

△ *The rich, red soil of Coonawarra (terra rossa) yields some of Australia's most flavourful Cabernet Sauvignons.*

side of the border) meant that few wine pioneers were willing to venture there. After all, there is little else to attract you to this frighteningly flat part of the world.

The first name associated with the region was that of the Penola Fruit Colony which sold low-alcohol red wine made with the Shiraz grape at the turn of the 20th century. Only one family, the Redmans, continued growing grapes and making wine for the next 50 years (they are still there); their wines were often sold to other producers elsewhere in the country. Some of these wines, notably the legendary Woodley's Treasure Chest series of reds from the late 1940s and early '50s, became well-known, but it was not until the early 1950s, when Melbourne restaurateur and wine merchant David Wynn purchased the cellars built by John Riddoch in 1891, that the region's true potential was recognised.

Wynn and his winemaker Ian Hickinbotham produced exceptional Cabernet Sauvignon and Shiraz wines: elegant, refined and long-lasting, fully deserving their 'Claret' or 'Hermitage' labels, and unusual at a time when the majority of Australian reds were rich and heavy 'burgundies'. This success attracted others to the area, and soon the ball was rolling. The larger companies such as Penfolds and Mildara came first, followed in the 1960s, '70s and '80s by the smaller producers.

Riesling quickly became the area's most widely-planted white grape; a reflection more of the historical importance of this variety than anything else. It still makes the odd good wine, but is being superseded by Chardonnay, which, because of Coonawarra's cool climate, can be satisfyingly intense and rich (and also makes good sparkling wine).

Cabernet Sauvignon still dominates as far as red varieties go, although some producers still maintain that the area is best suited to Shiraz. Recently, many winemakers have produced wonderful Merlots, and although it is still too early to predict anything with full confidence, this variety has the potential to do better here than almost anywhere else. Certainly Merlot and the other Bordeaux varieties of Cabernet Franc, Malbec and even Petit Verdot are adding superb complexity to the Coonawarra Cabernet Sauvignons.

The most important arguments in the region do not, however, revolve around grape varieties, they are all to do with land; the purists say that only vines planted on the narrow and clearly-defined strip of terra rossa should be entitled to the Coonawarra name while the more open-minded (read 'commercially-driven') say that the appellation should include some of the more fertile, black soils to the west.

One of the great ironies about all this is that Australian winemakers are traditionally dismissive of the French notion of terroir – and yet the terroir of Coonawarra is exactly what they are trying so hard to define and defend.

This relatively small patch of deep red earth was first hailed as perfect for growing fruit back in the 1860s. In the subsequent century it has evolved as an ideal vine zone yet it measures only 15 by 1.5 kilometres in size altogether; a tiny area for so much concentrated viticultural energy and passion. Perhaps a greater irony is that Coonawarra is not the only place in South Australia blessed with terra rossa. Many other strips of red soil over limestone are being discovered – and some may one day make even better wine.

Riverland

Some 240 kilometres northeast of Adelaide and just in from the border with Victoria, the huge irrigated vineyards of the Riverland stretch for as far as the eye can see away from the Murray River, the landscape broken by huge, refinery-like wineries. This is the guts of the Australian wine industry.

The vineyards and wineries of the Riverland, and those of northwest Victoria, produce most of Australia's everyday glugging wine, sold in bag-in-box casks, cheap bottles, or exported in bulk. More than any other, this region has inspired a change in Australian culture with beer-drinkers being wooed away to wine over the past decades to the extend that Australians now consume twice as much wine per capita as the average Briton.

Every style from sparkling to sweet is made here, with the abundant sunshine, almost inexhaustible water, and fertile soils providing the ideal conditions for growing large crops of healthy grapes.

It is easy for wine snobs in trendy Melbourne or Sydney bistros to be dismissive of the Riverland, but that attitude ignores how important this region has been, and continues to be, in providing the industry's vinous bread and butter.

Other Areas

As already mentioned, other viticulturally exciting spots have cropped up in South Australia in the last 30 years or so, the first, and still most important of which, is undoubtedly Padthaway.

This region is 80 kilometres to the north of Coonawarra, and equally remote. Its soils are more variable than its illustrious neighbour's (with similar red-brown loam to McLaren Vale predominating), while the cool climate is roughly the same. However the vines tend to require irrigation.

It is home to only a couple of estates, but is the site of many large-scale vineyards belonging to the major wine companies. Lindemans is the most famous of these, employing Padthaway Chardonnay (reliably full-flavoured and well-suited to barrel-ageing) in both regionally-designated wines and other multi-region blends. Seppelt and Hardy's are also represented and, like Lindemans, focus on white wines.

Chardonnay is undoubtedly Padthaway's greatest asset, although Sauvignon Blanc, botrytis-affected Riesling, elegant Cabernet and Merlot, and even spicy Shiraz have all found their way into the bottle over the years.

In the last five years or so, however, the focus has shifted from Padthaway somewhat, and turned towards other up-and-coming regions. At Koppamurra, just north of Coonawarra, and at Robe and Mount Benson, over on the South Australian coast, patches of red soil over limestone have been 'discovered', and thousands of acres of vines have been planted, mostly by the big companies. Early signs are very encouraging, with the young vines already producing wines of similar finesse to the best of Coonawarra.

These new regions will not be the last. Other places down here, along and inland from what has come to be called the Limestone Coast, are yet to be planted. The district's finest days – and finest wines – are perhaps yet to come.

△ *Above left: A close-up view of the source of Coonawarra's quality; a shallow layer of terra rossa over limestone.*

Victoria

Victoria's fortune was built on gold. It was gold that funded the grand architectural visions of Melbourne's new 19th-century aristocracy. It was gold that attracted thousands to the flourishing country towns of Bendigo Ballarat and Rutherglen. And it was the economic collapse that inevitably came after the gold ran out that put paid to Victoria's burgeoning wine industry reaching its full potential – that and an unhealthy dose of the vine louse phylloxera.

It was not until the 1980s that Victoria began to look once more like a real wine state, but Victorian winemakers have quickly made up for lost time, planting vineyards and opening cellar doors at a frantic pace.

Victoria has been ideally placed to take advantage of the rush to cool-climate viticulture over the last ten years. Australia's coolest mainland vineyards are found in this state, as are (not coincidentally) the bulk of Australia's premium sparkling wine facilities. The climate of some Victorian regions, particularly those south of the Great Dividing Range that sweeps down the east coast of Australia, compare favourably with the climate of Europe's finest wine districts – Burgundy in particular

But that's not to say everything is cool here: central and northeast Victoria can be as warm as the rest of the country, producing rich Shiraz and luscious liqueur Muscat to prove it. And the large irrigated vineyards and wineries in the hot far northwest of the state are home to the other half (with South Australia's Riverland) of the country's bulk wine production.

Yarra Valley and Geelong

The Yarra Valley, an hour's drive east of Melbourne, was Victoria's grand wine region of the 19th century. Settled by Swiss emigré aristocrats, and planted by the vineyard workers they brought with them from Switzerland, the place was a picturesque painting of sweeping vineyards and busy wineries in the late 1800s.

By the 1920s tastes had changed and the Yarra's vines had been replaced by sheep and cows. It was not until the 1970s that a few passionate and driven men, such as John Middleton at Mount Mary and Bailey Carrodus at Yarra Yering, brought attention back to the Yarra with the wines they were making from their small and well-managed vineyards.

More small wineries began popping up in the early 1980s, followed by medium-sized wineries, followed by larger operations and well-known names, such as Moët & Chandon's Green Point vineyards, and wine author James Halliday's Coldstream Hills. But the last five years have seen the real explosion, with three of the big four wine companies, Penfolds, BRL Hardy and Mildara Blass, buying wineries and planting vineyards. The Yarra has come of age.

The Yarra Valley can be split roughly into two different sub-regions (although there are pockets that do not fit comfortably into either): the cool undulating valley floor around Coldstream and Yarra Glen, characterised by grey loam soils; and the cooler, often higher area to the south around Seville, characterised by deep red volcanic soils.

This diversity makes the region a good one for producing a variety of wine styles, although the most successful to date have undoubtedly been restrained, tight Chardonnay, dark cherry-fruited Pinot Noir and elegant, well-structured Cabernet. Shiraz can grow well, in a peppery, medium-bodied style and still has its supporters, as do Sémillon (herbaceous and lean) and Sauvignon Blanc (minerally and juicy). As in Coonawarra, Merlot is showing some promising signs of greatness.

The land around Geelong, a small city to the south of Melbourne, was an even more substantial wine region in the last century than the Yarra Valley. Swiss vignerons settled here too, and by the 1870s had established large, ambitious vineyards. Unfortunately, the threat of phylloxera and misinformed government vine-pull schemes stopped the region reaching its potential.

The late 1960s saw the first tentative replanting of the area, by the Seftons at Idyll and Tom Maltby at the steep Mount Anakie vineyard. The region's best estate,

△ *Warm-climate vines at Morris in Rutherglen, northeast Victoria, home of velvety liqueur Muscat dessert wines.*

Bannockburn, was established next, and the ensuing years have seen a few others join them, notably, in the 1980s, Scotchmans Hill on the Bellarine Peninsula, jutting into Port Phillip Bay to the east.

Pinot Noir and Chardonnay are the region's best wines (both varieties benefiting from the long, cool growing season), with intensely spicy Shiraz bringing up the rear.

The Grampians and the Pyrenees

Although named after the dramatic mountainous outcrops to the west, the wineries of the Grampians region, two and a half hours' drive west from Melbourne, are actually scattered between the towns of Stawell, Great Western and Ararat. Indeed, Great Western used to lend its name to this wine district.

History is alive and well in Great Western. Walking through the miles of mould-covered tunnel cellars at Seppelt, you can feel it in the damp air, and smell it in your nostrils. These 'drives' were carved out in the 1860s by miners and it was down here, in perfect conditions, that Victoria's first great sparkling wines, made from the now-obscure varieties Ondenc and Chasselas, were matured in the late 19th century.

Those first wines cemented Great Western's reputation for sparkling wines, and by the middle of this century, the name had become synonymous for bubbly. Today, Seppelt Great Western is home to the sparkling wine production facility for the whole Southcorp group (which includes Penfolds, Lindemans, Seaview and Seppelt), with fruit and wine trucked here from across the country to be blended, tiraged, disgorged and bottled. Today, of course, these wines are made from the classic Champagne triumvirate, Chardonnay, Pinot Noir and Pinot Meunier.

The Grampians region is also a great place for table wines, most notably Shiraz in a concentrated style (with the wine from Mount Langi Ghiran showing alluring spice, and the century-old vines of Seppelt and Best's adding great depth), and surprisingly full but crisp Riesling. Great Western is also the spiritual home of sparkling red: ripe Shiraz put through the *méthode champenoise*, and one of Australia's great gifts to the world of wine.

An hour's drive over the Great Dividing Range to the northeast of Ararat leads to western Victoria's other main wine region, the Pyrenees, centred around the towns of Avoca and Moonambel.

Wine was made here on a small scale last century, but the area's modern history really starts in the 1960s, when French giant Rémy Martin established Chateau Rémy vineyards, initially to make brandy, moving swiftly to sparkling wine, and then into table wine (the vineyard and winery are now known as Blue Pyrenees Estate).

Other producers followed in the 1970s, all small, family-owned operations, with the exception of the larger Taltarni, and all makers of often heroically-proportioned red wines. Cabernet Sauvignon and Shiraz are undoubtedly the stars in this fairly warm region producing red wines with dense, earthy fruit and sometimes daunting tannins. Sauvignon Blanc and Chardonnay can yield impressive white wines on occasion.

North East Victoria

Rutherglen, up near the border with New South Wales, was Victoria's most important wine region during most of the last 100 years, providing huge quantities of fortified wines and full-blooded reds both to the domestic and UK markets. The elaborate Victorian mansions and often grand wineries of the area (the one at All Saints was built as a castle no less) are a testament to this.

The secret of the area's success lies in its relative warmth: red varieties such as Shiraz and the regional speciality Durif (originally a southern French hybrid) have no trouble ripening here, and produce wines of deep colour, fearsome tannins and high alcohol content.

But the region's fortified wines, especially liqueur Muscat and Tokay, continue to be Rutherglen's greatest assets. Made from ultra-ripe and raisined brown Musdcat grapes, the best of these wines are produced by descendants of the original 19th-century winemakers – names such as Campbell, Morris and Chambers point to their British ancestry – and are the product of many years maturation in barrel. They have

△ *Vines at Rhymney Valley Vineyard in western Victoria, where a temperate climate gives good acidity in grapes for sparkling wine.*

almost unparalleled richness, lusciousness and concentration, and with the market for premium fortified wine steadily decreasing, they represent exceptional value for money and are well worth trying.

Names can confuse here – the wine called liqueur Muscat is made with Muscat de Frontignan, while Tokay has no Hungarian or Alsace associations, being made with Muscadelle, another member of the Muscat grape family.

One of the northeast's oldest wineries, Brown Brothers at Milawa, south of Rutherglen, has also long been one of its most progressive. Brown Brothers stuck to its guns during the middle years of this century and continued to produce table wines when all but the local Italian tobacco growers wanted fortified wines. Indeed, it was Brown Brothers' move into the cooler King River Valley and up into the area now known as the High Country, to a height of some 750 metres, that partly inspired the many vineyards currently there.

These areas – the King Valley, and High Country – are the new face of northeast Victoria. Here the emphasis is on table and sparkling wine, with the aromatic white varieties such as Sauvignon Blanc and Gewürztraminer and even dry Muscat, and the perennial favourites Chardonnay and Pinot Noir (often used for sparkling wine) particularly impressing so far. Most of this fruit ends up in other wineries' blends, but this area is one to watch.

Goulburn Valley and Central Victoria

Until the ultra-modern Mitchelton operation arrived in the late 1960s, the Goulburn Valley, about two hours' drive north of Melbourne, was home to only one major winery: Chateau Tahbilk. Established in 1860, this wonderful old family-owned winery still produces wines much in the same way as it has done for the past century or so – wines that sum up in one fell swoop what the region does best: full-blooded reds. Tahbilk still has some original Shiraz vines from the 1860s. Whites are represented by an intense and quite long-lived Riesling, and by the regional speciality, Marsanne.

Mitchelton is still really the only other player in the area, and its approach is uncompromisingly modern. Mitchelton's Marsanne, for example, is treated to lavish new oak, whereas Tahbilk's is unwooded and crisply fragrant; and its Shiraz, taking full advantage of the warm climate, is rich and supple, whereas Tahbilk's is austere, tannic, and needs time in the bottle.

The wine regions of Bendigo and Heathcote, to the west of the Goulburn Valley, are similarly warm, being on the northern side of the Great Dividing Range, and the most successful wines here are also red. As in many other parts of Victoria, gold prospecting and viticulture both flourished here in the 1860s, but by the turn of the century, both had disappeared.

All of the wineries in Bendigo and Heathcote are small, and all are newcomers, starting in 1969 with Balgownie. In a relatively short period, these wineries have forged a reputation for brilliant, concentrated Shiraz and Cabernet Sauvignon (and even blends of the two). Brown sandy loam soils predominate, as they do in Goulburn, and the best wines, often Shiraz from unirrigated vineyards, have an utterly distinctive and appealing minty edge to their ripe, black-fruit flavours.

Ballarat, to the southwest of Bendigo, is another old gold town. Here, fairly high up in relatively cool conditions, the sparkling wine company of Yellowglen was established in the 1970s. Since then only a handful of small wineries have joined it, but this area may expand in the future.

North West Victoria

Starting at the town of Mildura up in the far northwest of the state, huge, hot, flat vineyards irrigated by the mighty Murray River stretch down through Robinvale and peter out around Swan Hill, picking up again in a smaller way near Echuca.

These vineyards and their attendant enormous wineries are the Victorian half of the guts of Australia's industry (see also South Australia's Riverland and New South Wales' Riverina). A hundred years ago this was an area for dessert wine and brandy production. In Mildura, the Mildara winery produced oceans of Australian 'sherry', some of it excellent, but table wines were non-existent.

Irrigation, introduced at the turn of the century, made a vital difference. Today, for instance, the name Mildara is synonymous with reliable quality wines. Without water, the area would not be able to produce its large crops of clean, ripe, healthy grapes, perfect for the cheap, everyday, fruity wines that continue to cement Australia's enviable reputation across the world.

Mornington Peninsula

The Mornington Peninsula could not be further in scale or style from the broad-acre vineyards and refinery-like wineries of the northwest. Here, on the tongue of land that curls down southeast of Melbourne into the bay, a surprisingly large number of small weekend vignerons (doctors, lawyers and dentists for the rest of the week) have joined a few larger professional wineries to push cool-climate viticulture and boutique winemaking to the limits.

Vineyards appeared here in earnest in the early 1970s, after a couple of small-scale false starts in the 19th century and the 1940s, and since then the number of producers has grown at a frightening rate. The region has something in common with the Yarra Valley in terms of the wine it produces but Mornington wines are usually more delicate.

The flat land around Dromana, near the sea, is the warmest part of the Peninsula, and manages to ripen Cabernet Sauvignon successfully – even if the wines still display an attractive leafiness. The red soils and altitude up on Red Hill are better-suited to Chardonnay and Pinot Noir (often used for sparkling wines), and the in-between climate on the eastern side of the Peninsula at Merricks seems to be good for all three. Shiraz, from a couple of suntrap vineyards (notably Paringa Estate) can be attractively intense and spicy.

Some of Victoria's best small winemakers, such as Stonier's and Dromana Estate, are here, but so far the cool climate and the high land prices have kept the larger wine companies at bay. They will buy in grapes in a good year, but they seem unlikely to establish a winery.

△ *Dramatic gum trees mark the Mount Langi Ghiran winery in Great Western, renowned for quality Rhône-style Shiraz red wines.*

Macedon Ranges and Sunbury

Victorian cool-climate viticulture reaches new heights in the hilly, windswept region of Macedon, one hour's drive north of Melbourne. Here, the vintage can come so late that some varieties have difficulty fully ripening. Not surprisingly then, the early-ripening varieties Chardonnay and Pinot Noir often make the best wines, with excellent estate-produced sparkling wines a regional speciality. The wineries of Kyneton, to the north, now considered a sub-region of Macedon, can be more successful with Shiraz and blends including Cabernet Sauvignon.

All of Macedon's wineries are new: the oldest was established in 1968. At Sunbury, a warmer (but still relatively cool) region to the south, between Macedon and Melbourne, winegrowing has a history stretching back to the 1860s. Sunbury is home to two splendid old Victorian bluestone wineries, one of which, Craiglee, makes some of the state's most wonderfully spicy, perfectly poised Shiraz.

Other Areas

Victoria is also home to dozens of wineries that either don't fall into recognised wine regions, or make up very loose, diverse regions that are united more by convenience than geography or wine character. There are, for example, a number of wineries far to the east of Melbourne grouped under the single heading of Gippsland, even though the two best ones, Nicholson River and Bass Phillip, are 160 kilometres from each other (the first making some of Australia's best Chardonnay, the latter its best Pinot Noir – both in minute quantities).

Similarly, a small number of vineyards have been established in the far southwest of the state, notably Crawford River and Seppelt's Drumborg vineyard. These are uncompromisingly cool sites producing similarly uncompromising, steely Riesling, good sparkling wine and herbaceous Cabernet Sauvignon.

Running up through the state towards New South Wales are a handful of small, high-altitude wineries that, while not falling into an easy region, nonetheless make great wine; look out for Chardonnays from Giaconda and Rieslings from Delatite..

Western Australia

Western Australia accounts for only a tiny proportion of Australia's wine production, but what it lacks in volume it more than makes up for in quality. The wineries and vineyards are clustered in regions scattered around the far southwestern edges of this enormous state, and despite the fact that they are often hundreds of kilometres apart, blending between them is common – even, in some cases, desirable. It is also not unheard of for West Australian grapes to be trucked across to the eastern states to make their way into blends, such is the quality of fruit that can be grown here.

Western Australia's best wine districts have, in a relatively short space of time, established strong and exciting reputations for wines with distinctive regional qualities – Margaret River Cabernet Sauvignon and Great Southern Riesling spring effortlessly to mind. This matching of variety and region is increasingly taking hold across the country: almost gone are the days when every small producer would try to be all things to all people, making everything from 'champagne' to 'port'. Specialisation is now the name of the game.

Western Australia is also a constant reminder of just how enormous Australia is, and how diverse its wine regions can be. When you consider that Perth is as far from Sydney as Moscow is from London, it comes as no surprise to find that vintage conditions in Western Australia each year can have nothing in common with vintage conditions in the eastern states.

Swan Valley, Perth Hills and Geographe

Western Australia's wine industry started in the early 19th century in the Swan Valley, a hot region to the north of Perth. Two of the district's best existing wineries, Houghton (also Western Australia's largest) and Sandalford, date from this period. With the hot climate and predominantly deep, free-draining soils, growing ripe grapes is easy, and for most of the last 150 years, the Swan Valley has turned these grapes into rich red

△ *Scene of a memorable film, the dramatic outline of Hanging Rock rises above vineyards of the same name in Macedon, Victoria.*

or fortified wines. Surprisingly though, the area's best and best-known wine is white: the famous Houghton White Burgundy, these days known as HWB, a Chenin Blanc-dominant blend with attractive fruit, which also ages well into honeyed richness.

To the east of Perth, up in the hilly country of the Darling Ranges, a host of relatively new wineries are producing wines that benefit from the slightly cooler climate. And stretching from south of Perth down almost to Margaret River is a diverse band of wineries loosely huddled under the regional name of Geographe, or South West Coastal Plain. Although all share the same grey sandy soil, the climate of each vineyard varies, growing steadily cooler as you travel south. Chardonnay, Riesling and elegant reds have been produced successfully here.

Margaret River

The Margaret River wine region owes its existence more to rational scientific thought than to romance or tradition. It was established in the late 1960s because a study of potential viticultural areas concluded it would be a great place to grow grapes, finding similarities between its soils and climate and those of Bordeaux. Having said that, though, the natural beauty of Margaret River is enough reason in itself to settle here.

The climate of this region, 320 kilometres south of Perth, is indeed wonderfully suited to making good wine, as the many who now do so will testify. It is neither too warm nor truly cool, and a wide variety of grapes grow well here.

In keeping with a longstanding Australian tradition – remember Dr Penfold and Dr Lindeman – the first to plant vines and make wine here were doctors: Dr Cullity at Vasse Felix, Dr Pannell at Moss Wood and Dr Cullen at Cullen. These three made some of the best Cabernet Sauvignons ever to be seen in Australia, and many other new winemakers soon followed.

Today, Margaret River is home to some of the biggest names in the industry – although most of them are anything but large in terms of production. Cabernet Sauvignon, either on its own or blended with Merlot and/or Cabernet Franc, is still the area's biggest drawing card, making wines of pure blackcurrant fruit, firm, tight structure and, with some bottle age, a magical complexity. More recently, Chardonnay has carved a niche for itself here, producing wines with enormous intensity and lingering richness – although, to be fair, the Chardonnays of Leeuwin Estate have been brilliant since the early 1980s.

Other successful wine styles here include crisp, juicy, herbaceous Sémillon, often blended with Sauvignon Blanc, peppery Shiraz and, at Cape Mentelle, the best of the few Zinfandels made in Australia.

Great Southern

This huge region, encompassing a number of vineyards scattered across hundreds of square kilometres right on the southern edges of Western Australia, was also originally planted as the result of a viticultural study. Tentatively at first in the mid-1960s, then with more conviction from the 1970s on, vineyards and wineries began to appear around Mount Barker, Frankland, Denmark and Albany – each many kilometres from the other, but all with fairly similar grey-brown loamy soils.

Climate varies markedly from sub-region to sub-region – with the cool influence of the sea at Denmark and Albany on the coast obviously having no effect at Mount Barker further inland – but all the vineyards are regarded as fairly warm.

As you would expect in a new region, a wide variety of grapes have been planted and trialled, and some have performed better than others. The best and most distinctive so far is Riesling, which is more reserved and less limey than, say classic Clare Riesling, but has a similar capacity to age gracefully.

Pinot Noir has been highly successful in isolated spots, Cabernet Sauvignon is amongst the most elegant in the country and, more recently, Shiraz has impressed, with often startlingly close approximations of wines from the Rhône Valley.

Other Areas

As in South Australia, Western Australia continues to unearth new wine regions, and there is plenty of land still to be tried.

The latest is Pemberton, half-way between Albany and Margaret River. This cool region, spectacularly set against the Karri gum trees, is home to a small number of brand-new small wineries, and a larger number of huge vineyards planted by the big companies – notably Houghton in the Swan Valley. It is early days yet, but Chardonnay and Pinot Noir have both shown promise.

Who knows where in the West will crop up next?

Queensland/Northern Territory

They were a zealous lot at times, Australia's 19th-century wine pioneers. A few of them even set up vineyards in the unquestionably hot southern reaches of Queensland. Not for nothing is Queensland called the Sunshine State. These early vineyards at Roma formed the hottest, sunniest wine district in the country. Even

△ Vines mix with sheep at Cullens in the Margaret River region, Western Australia; the winery is known for excellent Chardonnay.

today, only Alice Springs, in the middle of the desert in the Northern Territory is hotter.

When in the late 1960s and early '70s this century's Queensland vignerons established their wineries, they chose a spot further south than Roma, just over the border from New South Wales. Here, in the region called Granite Belt, the summer heat is mitigated by the fact that the vineyards are high up: 700 metres and more above sea-level. Still, with the excessive sun and the vintage-time rains, it is hard to grow grapes well in Queensland, and the state's wines are seen as something of a curiosity. The most successful variety so far has been Shiraz which, at its best from producers such as Ballandean Estate, can be spicy, rich and intense.

And then there is Chateau Hornsby. This one-off winery at Alice Springs, slap bang in the middle of the hot red centre, was established 20 years ago and claims to be the first in the world to start picking, on the first day of January each year. Only in Australia, you could argue, would somebody even bother.

Tasmania

Tasmania is the smallest wine-producing state in Australia (apart from Queensland), with only about 2,000 tonnes of grapes crushed across the entire island each year – as opposed to about 900,000 tonnes nationwide.

The vineyards are situated in five small, disparate regions: Piper's Brook and Tamar Valley in the north near Launceston; around Hobart in the south; and on the east coast, at Coal River and near Freycinet Peninsula. The vineyards in the north are marginally warmer than those near Hobart, but all are at the edge of cool-climate viticulture. Soils vary widely from red volcanic through sandy to dark alluvial, and wind can be a problem across the state.

Tasmania's first vineyards were planted way back in the 1820s, and it was from Tasmanian nurseries that many of the vine cuttings came to establish the wine

industries of both South Australia and Victoria. But by the time those other two states were flourishing, Tasmania's wine industry had disappeared, due in part to the undeniably cool conditions of the place. The first vineyards of modern times were planted in the 1950s, notably at Moorilla Estate, near Hobart, but the first to really exploit the potential of Tasmania was Piper's Brook Vineyard in the early 1970s.

In a move reminiscent of the establishment of Margaret River in Western Australia, viticultural scientist Andrew Pirie had made an extensive study of Australia and settled upon the Piper's Brook region as most closely resembling some of France's better districts – so he planted there, and began to make wine. The success of Pirie's Piper's Brook wines has encouraged many others. The relatively large vineyards and winery of Heemskerk soon followed, and today both a host of small estate producers and a number of vineyards providing fruit for mainland companies make up the Tasmanian industry. In all, there are more than 50 wineries selling wine commercially.

Wines here inescapably display their cool-climate origins. Sparkling wine, although a relatively recent development, is one of Tasmania's most successful wine styles, with the long, cool growing season producing fruit and wine with excellent crisp natural acidity. Not surprisingly, much of the fruit grown here for mainland companies is also destined for the increasingly popular sparkling wine. The cooler climate is perfect for Riesling, Gewürztraminer and Pinot Gris, all of which have a steely crispness and ability to age well; and botrytised Rieslings, which, while scarce, have been excellent. The ubiquitous Chardonnay has of course established itself in Tasmania as firmly as it has everywhere else, producing wines with tangy, peachy flavours and often mouthfilling richness.

Although Cabernet Sauvignon was initially the main focus for reds in this state, and, in better years, can produce attractive – if leafy – light-bodied wine, Pinot Noir has since superseded it as a far more suitable variety. At its best, from the Piper's Brook region, and some vineyards on the east coast, it can make wines with deep cherry fruit and spicy complexity.

△ Above left: Denis Hornsby surveys his vineyard at Alice Springs. Above right: Tasmania's cool climate is reflected in its crisply acidic quality sparkling wines.

Recommended Producers

New South Wales

Lower Hunter

Brokenwood – Small, high-quality producer, making great Hunter Sémillon (Cricket Pitch) and Shiraz (Graveyard).

Lake's Folly – The region's first new winery of modern times (built in the 1960s), still producing elegant Cabernet Sauvignon and complex Chardonnay.

Lindemans – Historically a Hunter-based company, now making wine in all three major states: good, traditional Sémillon and Shiraz in the Hunter; fine wines from Padthaway and great Coonawarra reds; as well as good value multi-regional blends, the most famous of which is Bin 65 Chardonnay.

McWilliams Mount Pleasant – Again, traditional Hunter wines: earthy Shiraz and glorious Sémillons, released with a few years' bottle age.

Tyrrells – Family-owned, fairly large winery, justifiably famous for Australia's first commercial Chardonnay, Vat 47, which is still among the country's best.

Upper Hunter

Rosemount Estate – Big, family-owned producer, based in the Upper Hunter but making a vast range of wines from across southeastern Australia, the best of which are often Upper Hunter Chardonnay (Roxburgh), McLaren Vale Shiraz (Balmoral) and Chardonnay from Orange, central New South Wales.

Mudgee

Huntington Estate – Dense and flavour-packed Cabernet Sauvignon and Shiraz from one of Mudgee's smaller producers.

Montrose – The area's biggest winery, now owned by Orlando-Wyndham, producing good wines, notably thick Shiraz.

Riverina

De Bortoli – Producer of value-for-money quaffers, as well as Australia's undisputed 'first growth' dessert wine, the wondrous botrytised Sémillon Noble One. Also has a good winery in the Yarra Valley, Victoria, making premium cool-climate wines.

South Australia

Adelaide Plains

Barossa Valley Estate – Good value wines sold under the BVE label; ultra-premium, concentrated Shiraz under the E&E label.

Primo Estate – Vibrant young wines under the Primo label and serious reds (such as Amarone-style Cabernet Sauvignon/Merlot) under the Joseph label.

Adelaide Hills

Lenswood Vineyards – Tim Knappstein (ex-Clare Valley) now makes superb Sauvignon Blanc, Chardonnay and Pinot Noir in the Adelaide Hills.

Petaluma – From here, winemaker Brian Croser makes top-class sparkling wine and Chardonnay using Hills fruit; plus a stunning Riesling from vineyards at Clare and great reds from Coonawarra.

Shaw & Smith – Flying winemaker Martin Shaw and Australia's first Master of Wine, Michael Hill-Smith produce crisp Sauvignon Blanc and rich Chardonnay.

Barossa Valley

Charles Melton – Best for rich, mouth-coating Barossa Shiraz and a vaguely Rhône-like Grenache/Shiraz/Mourvèdre blend, Nine Popes.

Orlando – Big producer, best known for huge-selling Jacob's Creek brand (a multi-regional blend), but also making good wines from Coonawarra, Eden Valley and elsewhere.

Penfolds – Australia's best-known wine company, specialising in reds – from the humble Koonunga Hill to the great 707 Cabernet Sauvignon and mighty Grange Shiraz – also beginning to do well with white wines.

Peter Lehmann – One of the great characters of the Barossa, Peter Lehmann makes some of the region's best wines, both red and white.

Rockford – Small, almost cult-like winery, making super-concentrated Basket Press Shiraz and wonderful sparkling Black Shiraz.

St Hallett – Another top red wine producer with Old Block Shiraz, from ancient, low-yielding vines, at the top of the list.

Yalumba – Old winery, making dazzling array of wines, from good budget fizz, Angas Brut, to premium, big Barossa reds. Also has excellent vineyards Pewsey Vale and Heggies in the cooler Eden Valley.

Eden Valley
Henschke – Traditional winery, well-known for complex, earthy reds, the most famous of which is Hill of Grace. Also has good vineyards in the Lenswood district of the Adelaide Hills.

Mountadam – Pioneer in Australia in the 1970s of cooler-climate, serious Pinot Noir and Chardonnay.

McLaren Vale
Chapel Hill – Excellent Riesling from Eden Valley, Shiraz from McLaren Vale, and Cabernet Sauvignon from Coonawarra (the last two often blended).

D'Arenberg – Formerly a stoutly traditional producer of rustic, long-lived reds; has now widened its range and improved quality.

Hardys – Famous old-established producer, making everything from sparkling wine to classic, rich, chocolatey Eileen Hardy Shiraz.

Mount Hurtle – Famous flying winemaker Geoff Merrill produces a range of elegant, serious wines under his own name, and fruit-packed, well-balanced wines under the Mount Hurtle label.

Seaview – Extremely good-value red, white and sparkling wines (most of which are multi-regional blends), plus Edwards & Chaffey premium range, made from McLaren Vale fruit.

Wirra Wirra – Producer of sturdy reds, almost European in style, with finesse and complexity behind the ripe fruit.

Clare
Grosset – Small but brilliant maker of stunningly intense Riesling, great Chardonnay and Pinot Noir (from Adelaide Hills fruit) and a tight Cabernet Sauvignon blend. Tim Knappstein worked here and his legacy is still apparent in the wines.

Leasingham – Revitalised Clare winery with large vineyard holdings and good wines; Riesling and Shiraz are the most impressive examples.

Sevenhill – Made by Jesuit brothers, the wine here (especially Riesling and a red blend including Shiraz and Malbec) can be some of the region's best.

Wendouree – Tiny, much sought-after producer making red wines of almost impossible concentration and staying power from a small, old vineyard.

Coonawarra
Bowen Estate – Makes some of the region's most generous wines, combining Coonawarra finesse with masses of ripe fruit.

Katnook – Fairly large producer, doing well with Cabernet Sauvignon and Merlot, but also often excelling with Sauvignon Blanc.

Mildara – Huge company with vineyards here in Coonawarra that can produce great Cabernet Sauvignon.

Penley Estate – Ex-Penfolds winemaker Kym Tolley makes some of the region's best Cabernet Sauvignon: extremely concentrated, rich and opulent.

Wynns – The best-known Coonawarra producer, making commendable wines across the board, from good-value, white-label Shiraz, to monumental flagship wines: John Riddoch Cabernet Sauvignon and Michael Shiraz.

Victoria
Yarra Valley
Coldstream Hills – Wine writer James Halliday's dream winery come true, producing great Chardonnay, Pinot Noir and Cabernet Sauvignon.

Green Point (Domaine Chandon) – Champagne house Moët & Chandon's Australian winery makes some of the country's best sparkling wine.

Mount Mary – One of the wineries responsible for the Yarra's renaissance: elegant, complex Cabernet Sauvignon and sometimes brilliant Pinot Noir.

Oakridge Estate – Big, impressively complex Cabernet Sauvignon, often the Yarra Valley's best.

Tarrawarra – Pinot Noir and Chardonnay specialist, both wines made using 'Burgundian' techniques, and both invariably excellent.

△ *John Duval: top winemaker at Penfolds in the Barossa Valley, South Australia.*

Yarra Yering – Another renaissance winery. The reds, in particular the Cabernet Sauvignon blend Dry Red No 1, are among Australia's most concentrated.

Geelong

Bannockburn – For many years a producer of top-class sturdy Pinot Noir and delicious Chardonnay, now also successful with spicy, peppery Shiraz.

Scotchmans Hill – New producer making good wines from local and bought-in fruit: Sauvignon Blanc and Pinot Noir are often the best of the range.

Grampians

Bests – Traditional winery owning some vines well over a century old. Shiraz can be extraordinarily intense.

Mount Langi Ghiran – Excellent producer with a varied output including peppery, rich Shiraz, full Riesling and good Pinot Grigio.

Seppelt Great Western – The region's showpiece winery with historic underground tunnels for maturing sparkling wine, which is the winery's speciality (along with insanely rich Shiraz). Seppelt owns another historic winery, Seppeltsfield, in the Barossa, where fortified wines are made.

Pyrenees

Blue Pyrenees Estate – Formerly Chateau Rémy, this winery now produces good sparkling wines as well as the European-styled Blue Pyrenees red blend.

Dalwhinnie – Tiny, family-run winery, with rich, oaky Chardonnay, bold Cabernet Sauvignon and taut, brambly Shiraz.

Taltarni – The area's largest winery, making the whole range of wines from sparkling up, but excelling with often hugely tannic reds, especially Cabernet Sauvignon.

North East Victoria

Baileys – At Glenrowan, south of Rutherglen, this old winery makes the region's most luscious Muscat and Tokay, as well as heroically structured Shiraz.

Brown Brothers – Fairly large, family-run winery, with mind-boggling range of good wines, seemingly with almost every grape variety on earth represented.

Campbells – Produces some of the northeast's more reserved fortifieds, and some good new-style reds such as spicy Bobbie Burns Shiraz.

Morris – Staunchly traditional producer of big, hearty reds and dazzlingly complex and quite delicious liqueur Muscat.

Goulburn Valley

Chateau Tahbilk – Another historic, traditional winery, with tannic, long-lived reds and the wonderful, heady, and equally long-lived white Marsanne.

Mitchelton – Just across the Goulburn River from Tahbilk, this modern (1969) winery markets a wider range of wines, from good Riesling to exuberant Shiraz.

Central Victoria

Jasper Hill – Heathcote's best winery, making full, floral Riesling and dense, fragrant reds that are surprisingly drinkable while still young.

Yellowglen – The one major winery in the Ballarat region, to the west of Melbourne, it only produces sparkling wine – occasionally very well.

Mornington Peninsula

Dromana Estate – Produces excellent Cabernet Sauvignon and Chardonnay, and more recently a range of Italian varietals (Nebbiolo, Barbera) from bought-in grapes.

Stonier's – At their best, the reserve Chardonnay and Pinot Noir from Stoniers can be the region's top wines.

Paringa Estate – Tiny but excellent winery making the area's best Shiraz and some stunningly spicy Pinot Noir.

Macedon Ranges and Sunbury

Craiglee – Historic winery and vineyard making good wines, with poised, spicy Shiraz the best of the bunch.

Hanging Rock – Sparkling wine is the passion here, but other wines, particularly Shiraz brought in from Heathcote, also good.

Virgin Hills – Idiosyncratic winery that produces just one wine: a blend of many different red varieties that, when good, can be exceptional.

Western Australia

Swan Valley

Houghton – Western Australia's largest producer, making wines from local fruit and grapes trucked in from across the state. Also sells under the Moondah Brook label.

Sandalford – Likewise situated in the Swan Valley, but making multi-region blends, albeit on a slightly higher level.

Geographe

Capel Vale – Remote winery that has produced some outstanding wines, including steely Riesling and herby Cabernet Sauvignon.

Margaret River

Cape Mentelle – Successful at almost everything, with great Cabernet Sauvignon, Chardonnay, Zinfandel, Sémillon/Sauvignon Blanc and Shiraz. Also owns New Zealand's Cloudy Bay vineyard, famous for Sauvignon Blanc.

Cullen – Brilliantly dense and concentrated Cabernet Sauvignon, complex Chardonnay and unusual oak-aged Sauvignon Blanc from one of the region's best winemakers.

Leeuwin Estate – Chardonnay is the star at this showpiece winery: a multi-layered wine made from extremely low-yielding vines.

Moss Wood – Great Cabernet Sauvignon here, too, but in a more approachable, less tannic style than its neighbours.

Pierro – A fairly recent arrival, but already vying with Leeuwin for the top spot on the Chardonnay ladder.

Great Southern

Goundrey – An ambitiously large operation, but making some stunning wines, especially the excellent Shiraz and floral Riesling.

Howard Park – John Wade makes wine for many other Western Australia wineries, but his own Howard Park wines are often the best: excellent Cabernet Sauvignon and heady, fragrant Riesling.

Plantaganet – Sets the standard in this part of the world for Chardonnay (particularly unwooded) and intense, peppery Shiraz.

Wignalls – Almost alone down at Albany, and a consistent producer of wonderful, undergrowthy Pinot Noir.

Tasmania

Freycinet – Recently attracting a lot of attention for its rich and deliciously complex, spicy Pinot Noir.

Heemskerk – The sparkling wine, called Jansz, is easily the best wine from this winery, indeed the best of its kind in the state: crisp, appley and long.

Piper's Brook – Tasmania's premier winery, producing quite delicious wines across the range, from the 'Alsatian trio' of Riesling, Gewürztraminer and Pinot Gris, to leafy, elegant Cabernet Sauvignon.

△ *Dr Andrew Pirie, pioneer winemaker in Tasmania at Piper's Brook Vineyard.*

New Zealand

WHY ALL THE FUSS ABOUT KIWI WINE? It boils down to flavour. New Zealand is classified by viticulturists as having a 'cool climate' in which grapes are able to ripen slowly, retaining their fresh, lively acidity while building rich, concentrated aromas and flavours which flow through into the wines. New Zealand's Sauvignon Blancs are the most pungent in the world; its Chardonnays, Rieslings, Gewürztraminers and bottle-fermented sparkling wines are also notably fragrant and flavour-packed. The Cabernet Sauvignon, Merlot and Pinot Noir-based red wines often struggle to achieve full ripeness, but the finest display a delicacy more usually associated with French than Antipodean reds.

Sauvignon Blanc with a breathtaking intensity of crisply herbaceous flavour first swung the spotlight onto New Zealand wine in the 1980s, and since then the country's reputation has continued to soar. With only one per cent of world wine production, it is doing well to attract such attention.

▽ *Overlooking Lake Wanaka in Central Otago from the beautifully-situated Rippon Vineyard.*

Samuel Marsden, the Anglican missionary, made the first recorded planting of grapevines in New Zealand at Kerikeri, north of Auckland, in 1819. The country's earliest recorded winemaker, however, was Scotsman James Busby, first British Resident in New Zealand. When the French explorer Dumont d'Urville visited Busby at Waitangi in 1840, he was given 'a light white wine, very sparkling and delicious'. French priests and peasants, Hawke's Bay pastoralists, Dalmatian (Croatian) gum-diggers and others kept the flame ignited by Busby throughout the 19th century. But the assaults of oidium (powdery mildew), the vine-destroying phylloxera aphid and prohibitionist zealots together ensured that the early dreams of a flourishing antipodean wine industry faded.

The 1920s and '30s witnessed gradual but unspectacular growth in New Zealand's wine industry. It then boomed during the Second World War, when duties were raised on overseas wines. This growth continued during the 1950s and '60s,

thanks largely to lobbyist winemaker George Mazuran, president of the Viticultural Association. Mazuran won a string of concessions from successive governments during those years – a heavy reduction in the minimum quantities of wine that could be sold by winemakers and wine shops; approval for more retail outlets and licensing of restaurants to sell wine. These legislative breakthroughs laid the foundation for the industry's phenomenal growth rate of recent decades.

Yet fortified wines dominated New Zealand's output until the 1970s. Most Kiwis drank beer, and the few who enjoyed table wines opted for imported brands. Those prepared to buy the cheaper local product demanded strong, sweet 'sherries' and 'ports', typical hot-climate wines. After the Second World War, thousands of Kiwi soldiers returned from service in France and Italy with a basic appreciation of wine. As perceptions of wine as 'plonk' faded, the country's struggling winemakers were presented with a golden opportunity – an enthusiastic demand for table wines.

In 1960, New Zealand's total vineyard area of 388 hectares was most heavily planted in Albany Surprise, Baco 22A and Seibel 5455; all low-grade American labrusca or hybrid varieties offering little scope to the winemaker. To make the fruity, slightly sweet white wines then popular, growers turned to the early ripening, heavy cropping German grape, Müller-Thurgau, which by 1975 was the most extensively planted variety and retained its ascendancy for 15 years. But in the last decade, as New Zealanders gradually developed a thirst for quality dry wines (white and red), plantings of classic 'noble' European varieties, including Riesling, Chardonnay, Cabernet Sauvignon, Pinot Noir, Sauvignon Blanc and Merlot have gradually outstripped the more mundane Müller-Thurgau.

If a temperate climate that ripens grapes slowly, coaxing out their most subtle aromas and flavours, is New Zealand's chief viticultural asset, the climatic bugbear of the winemakers is excessive and ill-timed rainfall. Heavy autumn rains often retard grape ripening and encourage the onslaught of botrytis rot, especially in the northern Auckland and Waikato regions. As a result, in the past decade most new vineyards have been planted in the long, drier belt running down the east coasts of both islands from Hawke's Bay in the north to Canterbury in the south.

Many quality-orientated growers are also shifting away from the typically heavy, clay soils of Auckland, and rich fertile river flats of Gisborne and parts of Hawke's Bay, to stonier, freer-draining sites which can reduce vine vigour and advance fruit ripening. This has been coupled with intensive work in the vineyards – vine trimming, canopy division and leaf plucking – which has been highly effective in reducing disease problems and improving fruit ripeness.

New Zealand exported NZ$60 million worth of wine in the year to June 1996, principally to the UK, Australia, Sweden and Canada. Compare this to just ten years ago, when wine exports earned just NZ$3.9 million. New Zealand's wine industry is extremely regionalised: over 90 per cent of the grape crop is grown in just three regions: Marlborough, Hawke's Bay and Gisborne. In all, the vineyards span 1,000 kilometres, ensuring that New Zealand wines display pronounced regional differences. Compare a crisp Sauvignon Blanc from Marlborough with its gentler cousin from Hawke's Bay to appreciate the contrasts.

INTRODUCTION

△ *Sheep graze alongside vines in New Zealand's fertile Gisborne/Poverty Bay region, known for its white wines.*

Auckland/Northland

From the turn of the century, Auckland (with Hawke's Bay) was one of the dual heartlands of New Zealand wine. The region has since declined in importance with the dramatic shift south of vine plantings – today Auckland has just three per cent of the national vineyard – but many companies retain their headquarters here and the wine trail is still one of the most absorbing in the country.

Many of Auckland's wineries are clustered west of the city; at Henderson and around the rural townships of Kumeu, Huapai and Waimauku. Others are based on Waiheke Island, at Matakana, an hour's drive north of the city, and in South Auckland. Some of the biggest names in New Zealand wine – Corbans, Villa Maria, Nobilo, Babich, Delegat's, Matua Valley, Selaks, Coopers Creek, Collards, Kumeu River – are based in Auckland, typically drawing grapes from as far south as Marlborough in the South Island. Montana, another major producer, has its headquarters and a giant blending, bottling and warehousing complex in suburban East Auckland.

From sprawling Waiheke Island in Auckland's Hauraki Gulf – where the summer rainfall is lower and average temperatures are higher than on the mainland – flows a trickle of much-acclaimed Cabernet Sauvignon and Merlot-based red wine.

The thick-skinned grape varieties like Cabernet Sauvignon perform well in Auckland's warm, but often humid and rainy, climate. Several West Auckland wineries are producing impressive, estate-grown Chardonnays, oak-aged Sauvignon Blancs and Cabernet-based reds, triggering a resurgence of consumer confidence in this historic region.

Few wineries are based in the almost subtropical Northland region, some 150 kilometres northwest of Auckland, but in favourable vintages, robust, ripe and rich-flavoured Cabernet Sauvignon, Merlot and Syrah-based red wines are produced.

Waikato/Bay of Plenty

The Waikato shares Auckland's natural advantages (high temperatures and sunshine hours) and disadvantages (heavy soils, abundant rainfall and high humidity) for grape-growing. The several small wineries based here are an eclectic blend of upmarket boutiques and more humble producers.

The foundation of the government viticultural research station at Te Kauwhata in 1897 gave grape-growing an early boost, and in the early 1970s Cooks (now merged with Corbans and McWilliams wineries) erected a new, 'space age' winery. Cabernet Sauvignon, Chardonnay and Sauvignon Blanc are the most popular varieties here.

Vineyards are rare in the Bay of Plenty region, east of the Waikato, but two top wineries (Morton Estate and Mills Reef) are based there, obtaining their fruit from the more southerly region of Hawke's Bay.

Gisborne

Gisborne, strictly speaking, is not the name of a province but of the port city of the Poverty Bay lowlands. To refer to this important vineyard area as Poverty Bay, however, would seem like a misnomer. With its bountiful sunshine, fertile, deep soils and frequent autumn rainfall, Gisborne is a naturally productive region accounting for almost one-third of all New Zealand wine.

Grape-growing is concentrated on the rich, alluvial flats around Gisborne, with pockets further north at Tolaga Bay and Tikitiki, and to the south near Wairoa. The mountainous East Cape has only limited areas suitable for viticulture.

Friedrich Wohnsiedler, a German storekeeper-turned-winemaker, pioneered the Gisborne wine industry in the 1920s. The boom came in the 1960s, when large Auckland wineries encouraged local farmers to diversify into grape-growing on a contract basis, and by 1986 Gisborne ranked as the largest wine region in the country, with 36 per cent of all plantings. Today, it now trails Marlborough and Hawke's Bay as New Zealand's third-largest wine region, as new vineyards are planted in the less fertile, drier regions to the south.

△ *Rose bushes give early warning of disease in the vine; seen here in the idyllic setting of Milton Vineyard, Gisborne.*

In Gisborne, you'll see countless rows of Müller-Thurgau, Chardonnay and Muscat Dr Hogg vines sweeping across the plains, yielding heavy crops to feed the crushers at Montana's and Corbans' mammoth wineries in the Gisborne industrial zone, or to be trucked overnight to many of the Auckland-based wineries. Much of Gisborne's grape crop is used for low-priced cask and sparkling wines.

However, careful site selection and painstaking vineyard management have yielded a stream of outstanding, quality white wines. Packed with drink-young appeal, Gisborne's fragrant, vibrantly fruity, well-ripened and soft Chardonnays are its greatest gift to the wine world, with an outstanding record on the New Zealand show-judging circuit. The perfumed, pungently peppery Gewürztraminers can also be memorable. In contrast, the late-season Cabernet Sauvignon has enjoyed little success here, typically lacking colour and flavour depth, but a rivulet of richly flavoured Merlots is disproving the notion that Gisborne is strictly white wine country.

Hawke's Bay

Hawke's Bay is the aristocrat among New Zealand's wine regions. With more than 20 wineries (several with restaurants), it's easy to spend several days exploring the Hawke's Bay wine trail. Apart from its rich, slowly evolving Chardonnays, ripely herbal Sauvignon Blancs and top-flight Cabernet Sauvignon and Merlot-based reds, it also has a tradition of quality winemaking stretching back into the 19th century.

Viticulture has flourished in the Bay since 1851, when Marist missionaries planted the first vines near Napier. In the 1890s, several wealthy landowners – most notably Bernard Chambers of the Te Mata Station and Henry Tiffen at Greenmeadows, Taradale – experimented with winemaking using classic European varieties. A Spaniard, Anthony Vidal, who in 1905 converted a Hastings racing stable into his cellar, was the first to plunge into full-time commercial winemaking.

Today, visitors can unravel Hawke's Bay's absorbing viticultural history at several wineries including Vidal Estate, which still occupies the original site in St Aubyns Street East, Hastings; at the Te Mata winery, the oldest in the country, erected in

stages from the 1870s; and at Montana's The McDonald Winery, complete with a wine museum. The neighbouring Mission Vineyards at Taradale, established by the Catholic Society of Mary in 1851, is by far the oldest winemaking enterprise in New Zealand still under the same management.

Hawke's Bay's climate is typified by warm, sunny summers, moderate rainfall and a strong maritime influence. Indeed, in terms of levels of sunshine hours and temperatures, the city of Napier has a climate similar to Bordeaux. During summer, anti-cyclonic conditions can cause droughts, but easterly cyclonic depressions can also bring torrential autumn rains. On average, though, Hawke's Bay enjoys a markedly drier autumn than Gisborne.

Vineyards here are spreading like wildfire: between 1992 and 1995, plantings soared by over 40 per cent, with Chardonnay and Cabernet Sauvignon the two key varieties, followed by Müller-Thurgau, Sauvignon Blanc and Merlot. Most are planted on the sweeping Heretaunga Plains. The area offers fertile alluvial soils over gravelly subsoils which are deposited by the rivers and creeks draining the rugged inland Ruahine and Kaweka ranges. Within the plains, though, winemakers must choose their sites carefully: not all are suited to viticulture. The areas of fertile silty loams with a high water table, especially those between Hastings and the coast, encourage vigorous growth, but can yield heavy crops of unripe, poorly balanced grapes. Recently, many quality-conscious growers have ventured onto low-vigour sites in the Ngatarawa dry belt and the warm, free-draining gravel country around Gimblett Road, inland from Hastings.

Hawke's Bay is New Zealand's most important red wine region, capable of producing claret-style wines which display rich, concentrated, cassis and spice-evoking flavours and a scent reminiscent of fine bordeaux. Its closest rivals are, perhaps, the top Waiheke Island reds, which equal the region's Cabernet Sauvignon and Merlot-based wines at the top of the quality ladder, but the Hawke's Bay reds are produced in greater volumes and are typically more affordable.

Whites include weighty Chardonnay, with intense, grapefruit-like flavours, good

△ *Hawke's Bay is home to some of New Zealand's finest red wines. Planting began here in the late-19th century.*

acidity and an ability to mature well for several years. Sauvignon Blanc, less pungent than that of Marlborough, offers ripe, rounded, tropical fruit characters with an easy-drinking appeal, while the complex, barrel-fermented models are the most stylish in the country. A sprinkling of outstanding Rieslings, sweet whites, bottle-fermented sparkling wines and Pinot Noirs have also been produced in Hawke's Bay.

Wairarapa

Seductively perfumed and supple Pinot Noirs flow from the Wairarapa, the North Island's most southerly wine region. Substantial vineyards have recently been established around the town of Masterton, but almost all of the region's top wines to date have been grown near the once sleepy hamlet of Martinborough.

William Beetham, who first planted vines at his tiny Wairarapa vineyard in 1883, produced a 'Hermitage' (Syrah) praised in 1895 by Romeo Bragato, a viticultural expert, as being of 'prime quality'. The strong resurgence of viticultural interest in the Wairarapa came just under a century later, when Wellington scientists documented similiarities between Martinborough's climate and those of top French wine regions, particularly Burgundy. Now, two Burgundian varieties, Pinot Noir and Chardonnay, are the region's most widely planted grapes, but Cabernet Sauvignon, Sauvignon Blanc and Merlot, all Bordeaux varieties, cover an almost equal area.

Martinborough is the place to aim for in Wairarapa; the climate of warm summers and cool, dry autumns more closely resembles that of Marlborough across Cook Strait than Hawke's Bay in the north. Martinborough's white wines also display the tense acidity and clear flavours typical of Marlborough.

Red wine, though, is Wairarapa's most exciting success. Pinot Noir, which prefers free-draining soils, thrives in the pockets of shallow loams over gravelly subsoils which border and penetrate the township. The result: a consistent, intense varietal, yielding deeply scented and rich-flavoured wines. But this is a versatile wine region, with classy Chardonnay, Riesling, Gewürztraminer, Pinot Gris, Sauvignon Blanc and (less often) Cabernet Sauvignon also growing well.

Marlborough

In 24 exhilarating years since Montana planted the first vines, Marlborough has emerged as New Zealand's most important wine region. Almost 40 per cent of the country's vines are concentrated in the region, and of all New Zealand wine styles Marlborough Sauvignon Blanc is by far the most widely acclaimed around the world.

Cooler than Hawke's Bay, yet the warmest of the South Island's winelands, Blenheim, the main town in Marlborough, frequently boasts the highest total sunshine hours in the country. Warm, sunny days alternating with clear, cold nights and a fairly dry autumn give Marlborough grapes a long, slow, flavour intensifying ripening period. To counter the dehydrating effects on the vines of hot, dry northwesterly winds, most growers install trickle irrigation systems. Soils are variable, even within individual vineyards, with the less fertile, more shingly sites being the most sought after.

Sauvignon Blanc is the key to Marlborough's success – penetrating, herbaceous, with a leap-out-of-the-glass bouquet and explosion of zingy, gooseberry and green-capsicum flavour. Montana Marlborough Sauvignon Blanc, sold worldwide, and the prestigious Cloudy Bay are just two examples of the region's expertise in this field, and the larger Auckland-based wineries draw much of their Sauvignon Blanc fruit from Marlborough. There is, though, more than one string to Marlborough's vinous bow: the region also produces many of New Zealand's classiest Rieslings, Chardonnays, botrytised sweet whites and bottle-fermented sparkling wines.

For such an acclaimed wine region, Marlborough (or at least the Wairau Valley, where most of the vines are concentrated) is remarkably small. Rugged mountains, rising to almost 3,000 metres, straddle most of the region. The Wairau Valley runs 26 kilometres inland, but is just 14 kilometres wide at the eastern extremity, where it meets the sea at Cloudy Bay; this body of water is so called due to the silt that drains into it from the Wairau River after heavy rain.

The distance from the Wither Hills in the south to the towering Richmond Ranges on the Wairau Valley's northern flank is also anything but wide: just about ten

△ *Serried ranks of vines on the stony soil of Montana's Brancott Estate in the Marlborough region.*

kilometres. Plantings here have leapfrogged over the southeastern hills into the Awatere Valley, but a lack of irrigation has slowed down expansion.

The community of Marlborough wine producers is growing swiftly as overseas investment streams into the region. Australian winemakers recognised its potential as early as 1985, when David Hohnen of Cape Mentelle set up Cloudy Bay. European winemakers are also scattered around the region today; the Fromm winery was founded recently by Swiss immigrants Georg and Ruth Fromm to specialise in red wines, especially Pinot Noir.

Most conspicuous of all are the mounting links between Marlborough and the great houses of Champagne. Deutz Marlborough Cuvée is produced by Montana under the technical guidance of Deutz and Geldermann. Veuve Clicquot is now the majority shareholder in Cloudy Bay. Moët & Chandon, owner of Domaine Chandon in Victoria, Australia, is involved in masterminding the production of the excellent Domaine Chandon Marlborough Brut.

To call Marlborough Sauvignon Blanc country is an oversimplification. Almost two thirds of New Zealand's Sauvignon Blanc is planted here, and Sauvignon Blanc and Chardonnay together account for 54 per cent of all the region's vines. But Müller-Thurgau, Riesling, Cabernet Sauvignon, Pinot Noir (used mainly as a sparkling wine base), Sémillon (customarily blended with Sauvignon Blanc) and Merlot are also grown. Despite the generally disappointing performance of Cabernet Sauvignon, which in Marlborough can fail to achieve full ripeness, high hopes are held for the earlier-ripening Pinot Noir and Merlot.

Nelson

Over the ranges to the west of Marlborough lies Nelson, a small but growing wine region which is home to one of New Zealand's most distinguished wines: Neudorf Moutere Chardonnay. This beautifully hilly region enjoys Marlborough's advantages of warm summers and high sunshine hours, but as harvest approaches in March the risk of rain is higher. Vines are grown on the silty, windy Waimea Plains and in the heavier clay soils of the blue green Upper Moutere hills.

Just a trickle of wine was made in Nelson during the 19th century. The industry's key pioneers, however, were Austrian-born Hermann Seifried and his wife, Agnes, who planted their first vines in the Upper Moutere in 1974, and now own the region's only large winery.

Nelson is best known for its fragrant, fresh, tangy white wines, which display good flavour depth and vigour. Sauvignon Blanc, Riesling and Chardonnay are the three most popular grape varieties, but Cabernet Sauvignon and (more successfully) Pinot Noir are also well established.

Canterbury

This is one of the world's most southerly wine regions, and the industry has blossomed since the first commercial vineyard, St Helena, was planted at Belfast, north of Christchurch, in 1978. Today, Canterbury is New Zealand's fourth largest wine region, ahead of the Wairarapa and Auckland.

French peasants at Akaroa made the first Canterbury wines for their domestic tables in the mid-19th century. Just over 100 years later Dr David Jackson of Lincoln University triggered the revival of interest in Canterbury winemaking in 1973, by embarking on grape trials designed to pinpoint the most suitable varieties for the region's cool, dry viticultural climate.

Riesling, Chardonnay and Pinot Noir have flourished, leading to the foundation of over 20 wine companies. Most are grouped in two zones: in the undulating North Canterbury countryside around Waipara, where the stylish wines of Pegasus Bay are setting the pace, and on the pancake-flat plains surrounding the city of Christchurch.

Canterbury's fierce, hot 'nor'westers' dehydrate the vines in both districts, but the Teviotdale Hills protect Waipara's vineyards from the province's cooling easterly breezes. Waipara's best wines are thus typically more robust and rich in flavour than the leaner, racier wines from the south.

Central Otago

For dramatic scenery, nothing can beat Central Otago – a tiny wine region, but one that enjoys a high profile and a big reputation. The vines are grown at a high altitude here, and the climate is definitely cool, so a sunny, elevated, north-facing vineyard site with a low-frost risk is essential. Conditions here have been compared by many to those prevailing in fine German vineyards. However, exceptionally dry autumn weather (by New Zealand standards) usually allows the grapes to be left late on the vines, for an extended ripening period.

The few established wineries are based near Queenstown, at Alexandra and at beautiful Lake Wanaka. Vineyards planted recently at Bannockburn, near Cromwell, are also yielding impressively fragrant wines.

The finest wines flowing from Central Otago's majestic inland valleys are its richly varietal Pinot Noirs, but the scented, freshly acidic Rieslings are full of promise. The naturally high acid levels of the region's wines also suggest a strong future in bottle-fermented bubblies. Watch this space.

△ Left: Chard Farm, Central Otago; New Zealand's only ice wine is made here.
Right: Cool-climate vines flourish in this protected Queenstown valley.

Recommended Producers

Auckland/Northland

Babich Wines – Established in 1916, this medium-sized, family-owned winery has a reputation for modest pricing. It also produces some of the more stylish Hawke's Bay wines. Highlights of the range are the steely, slowly evolving Irongate Chardonnay, a robust, barrel-fermented Mara Estate Sauvignon Blanc and a concentrated Irongate Cabernet/Merlot.

Collard Brothers – Drawing fruit from the company-owned Rothesay Vineyard in West Auckland, Hawke's Bay and Marlborough, this medium-sized producer makes outstanding white wines. Look out for the bargain-priced Hawke's Bay Chenin Blanc, as well as a zesty Riesling from Marlborough and a strapping, intensely citrussy Rothesay Vineyard Chardonnay.

Coopers Creek – Winemaker Kim Crawford, a star performer at New Zealand wine shows, produces highly scented wines that drink well in their youth. The intensely aromatic, vibrantly fruity Riesling and mouthfilling, succulent Swamp Reserve Chardonnay from Hawke's Bay are recommended, backed up by fresh, vibrantly fruity Cabernet and Merlot.

Corbans Wines – New Zealand's second-largest winery, producing over 30 per cent of the country's wine, is controlled by the Dutch brewer Heineken NV. Corbans makes a huge array of wines under its Corbans, Cooks, Huntaway, Stoneleigh Vineyard, Robard & Butler and Longridge of Hawke's Bay brands. The lush, buttery Gisborne Chardonnays under the Corbans Cottage Block and Private Bin labels are pacesetters for the rest of the industry, and the piercing, tangy Rieslings from the Stoneleigh Vineyard in Marlborough are great value.

Delegat's Wine Estate – Jim and Rose Delegat, the only brother and sister team to head a major New Zealand winery, and winemaker Brent Marris, produce superb Hawke's Bay wines under the Delegat's Proprietors Reserve label, especially the exceptionally rich, toasty Chardonnay. Their Marlborough wines, branded as Oyster Bay, include a stylish, tropical fruit and cut grass flavoured Sauvignon Blanc and a lightly oaked, citrussy, crisp Chardonnay.

Goldwater Estate – A powerful, robust wine crammed with blackcurrant, spice and oak flavour, Kim and Jeanette Goldwater's Cabernet Sauvignon/Merlot blend ranks among New Zealand's greatest reds.

Kumeu River Wines – The opulent, softly seductive Kumeu Chardonnay and top-tier, single-vineyard Mate's Vineyard Chardonnay, which both possess a near-Burgundian power and richness, are the standout wines from this winery, run for many years by the Brajkovich family.

Matua Valley Wines – This dynamic winery produces a striking, creamy-smooth Chardonnay and concentrated, brambly Merlot and Cabernet Sauvignon-based red under its top Ararimu label. The brisk, flavour-packed Marlborough whites, labelled as Shingle Peak, offer fine value.

Montana Wines – The colossus of the New Zealand wine industry, producing about 40 per cent of all New Zealand wine, Montana is owned by a publicly listed company, Corporate Investments. The zesty, assertive Marlborough Sauvignon Blanc and stylish, delicately yeasty Lindauer Brut rank among New Zealand's greatest wine bargains and enjoy strong export demand. The Hawke's Bay-grown Church Road Chardonnay and Church Road Cabernet/Merlot are impressively rich, ripe and flavourful.

Nobilo Vintners – New Zealand's fourth-largest winery produces an internationally popular, slightly sweet, Müller-Thurgau-based wine, White Cloud: a sort of New Zealand-grown Blue Nun. Other mainstays of the range are the toasty, buttery-soft Chardonnays from Gisborne and the tangy, keenly priced Marlborough Sauvignon Blanc.

Selaks Wines Cnr. – With vineyards and a gleaming new winery in Marlborough, this long-established West Auckland company produces several memorable variations on the theme of Sauvignon Blanc, with none more arresting than the barrel-fermented Sauvignon Blanc/Sémillon.

Stonyridge Vineyard – Only a few hundred cases are produced each year but Stephen White's Larose Cabernet is arguably New Zealand's greatest red wine. Its intensity of ripe fruit is breathtaking, yet the wine retains cool-climate delicacy and finesse.

Villa Maria Estate – New Zealand's third-largest wine company, controlled by George Fistonich, also owns Esk Valley and Vidal Estate in Hawke's Bay. Villa Maria consistently achieves excellence and value throughout its (flagship) Reserve, Cellar Selection and Private Bin ranges. In the competition arena, the intensely citrussy, spicy, creamy Reserve Barrique-Fermented Chardonnay, the gloriously perfumed, honey-sweet Reserve Noble Riesling and the bold, dark, flavour-packed Reserve Cabernet-based reds are all glamour horses.

Waiheke Vineyards – It took only two vintages (1993 and 1994) for this fledgling winery's strapping, excitingly concentrated and multifaceted Te Motu Cabernet/Merlot blend to win a reputation as one of New Zealand's most esteemed (and pricey) reds.

Waikato/Bay of Plenty

Mills Reef Winery – The Preston family's sumptuous winery on the edge of Tauranga produces classy Hawke's Bay white wines under its middle-tier Reserve label, together with distinguished, bottle-fermented sparkling wines and an especially notable, superbly crafted, top-tier Elspeth Chardonnay, full of peachy flavour.

Morton Estate – Think Morton Estate, and it's hard not to think Chardonnay. From Hawke's Bay fruit, the company fashions its regular highly refined, tightly structured Black Label Chardonnay, as well as a more forward, citrussy and biscuity, barrel-fermented White Label Chardonnay that in top vintages offers superb value.

Rongopai Wines – In the old, rambling, former government viticultural research station, Tom van Dam produces locally grown and Hawke's Bay wines, winning acclaim for his treacly sweet whites, especially the ravishingly scented Reserve Botrytised Riesling and opulent Reserve Botrytised Chardonnay.

Gisborne

The Millton Vineyard – James and Annie Millton, New Zealand's best-known organic winemakers, produce white wines of rewarding quality. The lush, pineapple-ripe, slightly honeyed Chenin Blanc Dry and exquisitely perfumed Opou Vineyard Riesling are backed up by top-flight sweet whites and citrussy Chardonnays.

Hawke's Bay

Brookfields Vineyards – Peter Robertson adopts a low profile, but his bold, savoury Reserve Chardonnay and substantial 'Gold Label' Cabernet/Merlot rank among Hawke's Bay's most memorable wines.

C J Pask Winery – Chris Pask, who owns substantial vineyards in the arid, stony Gimblett Road area, and his winemaker, Kate Radburnd, produce a solid selection of whites and reds, with the elegant and concentrated Reserve Chardonnay the jewel in the crown.

Clearview Estate Winery – On a shingly, free-draining site right on the coast at Te Awanga, Tim Turvey and Helma van den Berg produce a hedonistic, muscular Reserve Chardonnay with bottomless flavour and a trio of powerful, exuberantly fruity Cabernet Sauvignon, Merlot and Cabernet Franc-based reserve reds.

Esk Valley Estate – A key part of the Villa Maria empire, Esk Valley produces voluptuous, silky Merlot-based red wines, a delicious, strawberryish, dry Merlot Rosé and The Terraces, a staggeringly good estate-grown blended red in which Merlot and Malbec are the principal ingredients.

Mission Vineyards – Most of this historic winery's wines offer solid, budget-priced drinking. The slightly sweet Rhine Riesling is cheap, fragrant and full-flavoured and the top range, labelled Jewelstone, features a punchy, excitingly weighty, intense and deliciously complex Chardonnay.

Ngatarawa Wines – Alwyn Corban, a scion of the famous wine family, produces characterful wines, with the stylish, citrussy, Glazebrook Chardonnay and gloriously scented, Riesling-based Glazebrook Noble Harvest as the pick of the bunch.

Stonecroft Wines – From his gravelly, free-draining vineyards west of Hastings, Dr Alan Limmer coaxes weighty, ripely flavoured white wines and sturdy, concentrated reds, notably New Zealand's first impressive Syrah – dark, rich, plummy and peppery, and sometimes distinctly reminiscent of a good Crozes-Hermitage.

△ *Organic winemaker James Millton of Millton Vineyard, Gisborne.*

Te Mata Estate Winery – This winery was founded by Bernard Chambers over a century ago, and now headed by the dynamic John Buck. Te Mata Estate is noted for a powerful and tautly structured Elston Chardonnay, and the seductively fragrant, rich and supple Awatea Cabernet/ Merlot, not to mention one of New Zealand's most prestigious reds, the extraordinarily elegant Coleraine Cabernet/ Merlot.

Vidal Estate – Founded early this century and acquired by Villa Maria in the 1970s, Vidal produces two of New Zealand's most arresting reds – the power-packed, spicy, cedary Reserve Cabernet Sauvignon and more voluptuous, deliciously plummy and minty Reserve Cabernet Sauvignon/ Merlot. Equally rewarding are the citrussy, toasty Reserve Chardonnay and gently oaked, tropical fruit-flavoured Reserve Fumé Blanc.

Wairarapa

Ata Rangi Vineyard – A tiny winery with a huge reputation, Ata Rangi produces outstanding Chardonnays and a mouthfilling, cherryish, beguilingly perfumed and velvety Pinot Noir.

Dry River Wines – No other small New Zealand winery can match Dry River for the excellence it achieves across so many varieties and styles. Their wines include Pinot Gris, Gewürztraminer, Riesling, Chardonnay, various sweet white wines and a Pinot Noir. These are immaculately made, intense, long-lived wines with a deservedly sky-high reputation.

Lintz Estate – Chris Lintz's unpredictable but impressive range includes a floral, tangy, bottle-fermented Riesling Extra Brut, an amber-hued, ultra-sweet Noble Selection Optima, and some sturdy, tannic, flavour-packed Cabernet-based reds.

Martinborough Vineyard – Winemaker Larry McKenna put Martinborough on the map with his stunning 1986 Pinot Noir, and this delectably rich and multi-faceted wine still ranks among the country's best red wines. The white wines include Chardonnay, Sauvignon Blanc and Riesling and are equally distinguished.

Nga Waka Vineyard – This small white-wine specialist produces a magnificently deep-scented and vibrantly fruity Sauvignon Blanc and steely, bone-dry, consistently classy Riesling and Chardonnay.

Palliser Estate Wines – Under its premium Palliser Estate label (which is easily confused with the second-tier label, Palliser Bay), this relatively large Martinborough winery produces stylish, piercingly flavoured Riesling and Sauvignon Blanc and a deliciously rich and mealy Chardonnay.

Te Kairanga Wines – One of Martinborough's largest wineries, Te Kairanga produces consistently satisfying Chardonnays and Pinot Noirs. The non-reserve wines are good, but the savoury, rich and tautly structured Reserve Chardonnay and bold, concentrated Reserve Pinot Noir are especially exciting.

Nelson

Neudorf Vineyards – With major trophies from New Zealand, Australian and British competitions sitting in the cupboard, there's no doubting the magical quality of Tim and Judy Finn's magnificently rich, savoury and creamy Moutere Chardonnay. The floral, racy Riesling, aromatic, penetrating Sauvignon Blanc and complex, tannic Pinot Noir are also impressive.

Seifried Estate – Hermann Seifried gained an early reputation for bargain-priced, stylish Rieslings, but recently his weighty, vibrantly fruity and lush Sauvignon Blancs and lemony, nutty, vigorous Chardonnays have also moved towards a centre-stage reputation. The wines are all fine value.

Marlborough

Allan Scott Wines and Estates – Allan Scott's Rieslings and Sauvignon Blancs are pure Marlborough – fresh, invigoratingly crisp and awash with flavour.

Cellier Le Brun – Daniel Le Brun, who founded the company in 1980, is no longer involved, but the toasty, mouthfilling, enticingly rich and yeasty Le Brun Vintage Methode Traditionnelle Brut and excitingly fragrant and deep-flavoured, all-Chardonnay Blanc de Blancs still rate among New Zealand's champion sparkling wines.

Cloudy Bay Vineyards – In the glass, the superstar Sauvignon Blanc lives up to its reputation, with a breathtaking surge of fresh, zingy, ripely herbaceous, downright irresistible flavour. The concentrated, long-lived Chardonnay is a classy wine, as is Pelorus, an exceptionally deep-flavoured, bottle-fermented sparkling wine.

Grove Mill Wine Company – Aromatic, incisively flavoured white wines flow from this well-respected winery, notably the ravishingly fragrant, delicate Riesling and the frisky, gooseberry and green pepper-flavoured Sauvignon Blanc.

Hunter's Wines – Hunter's thrillingly rich and vibrant Sauvignon Blanc and its Sauvignon Blanc Oak Aged stablemate are regional classics. The Chardonnay is also extremely commendable, with great delicacy and finesse.

Jackson Estate – Distinctively rich and ripe, tropical fruit-flavoured Sauvignon Blanc is Jackson Estate's chief claim to fame, but the robust, savoury Reserve Chardonnay, the yeasty and delicate bottle-fermented sparkling wine, labelled Jackson Vintage, and the botrytised sweet whites are all superb.

Lawson's Dry Hills – Greatest delights from this fast-rising star of the Marlborough wine scene are the bold, richly varietal Gewürztraminer, a powerful Chardonnay and a stylish, somewhat oak-influenced Sauvignon Blanc.

Nautilus Estate – The Nautilus brand is owned by the wine distribution company, Negociants. With its voluminous fragrance and pure, ripely herbaceous and zingy palate, the Sauvignon Blanc is a Marlborough classic. The non-vintage sparkling wine, Cuvée Marlborough, made with a high percentage of Pinot Noir, is fragrant, yeasty and smooth, and immensely drinkable.

Saint Clair Estate Wines – This relative newcomer (first vintage 1994) produces a consistently rich-flavoured and lush, piercingly aromatic Sauvignon Blanc, as well as a beautifully scented, ripe Riesling.

Vavasour Wines – The non-wooded Dashwood Sauvignon Blanc from this winery bursts with fresh, lively, herbaceous flavour in a distinctly cool-climate style, but Vavasour's greatest wine is its intensely concentrated, flinty, superbly sustained Single Vineyard Chardonnay, which was previously labelled as Reserve Chardonnay.

Wairau River Wines – Wairau River excels with a stunningly powerful and flavour-packed Sauvignon Blanc, a delicious marriage of fresh, tropical and nettley fruit characters underpinned by lively acidity.

Canterbury

Giesen Wine Estate – The region's largest winery produces a wide range of wines, notably the ravishingly full-bloomed, richly honied and steely Botrytised Riesling as well as a classy, concentrated, estate-grown Reserve Pinot Noir.

Pegasus Bay – Pegasus Bay's distinguished selection of North Canterbury wines features a lovely, citrussy Chardonnay; zingy, lemon/lime-flavoured Riesling, partly fermented in barrel; as well as an exotically flavoured Sauvignon/Semillon and a bold, dark, rich-flavoured, smoky Pinot Noir.

St Helena Wine Estate – Canterbury's oldest winery produces a low-priced, savoury, earthy Pinot Blanc that offers great value, and, in favourable vintages, a weighty, lemony, steely Reserve Chardonnay and a fragrant, rich, spicy Reserve Pinot Noir.

Central Otago

Chard Farm Vineyard – On a spectacular site in the craggy Otago interior, brothers Rob and Greg Hay produce fine quality Rieslings and Chardonnays and a Pinot Noir that abounds with vibrant, cherryish, spicy flavour and drink-young appeal.

Gibbston Valley Wines – Apart from its hugely popular restaurant, this pioneering winery also boasts a deliciously peachy and toasty Central Otago Chardonnay and a rich, plummy, concentrated and velvety Reserve Pinot Noir.

Rippon Vineyard – On a breathtakingly beautiful site on the edge of Lake Wanaka, Rolfe and Lois Mills produce a steely, appley Chardonnay which is inspired by the great wines of Chablis. They also make an alluringly perfumed, buoyant, richly flavoured Pinot Noir which is good enough to rival Martinborough's finest.

△ Winemaker Kevin Judd of Cloudy Bay, a world-class winery part-owned by Veuve Clicquot Champagne.

South Africa

VISITORS TO THE SOUTH AFRICAN VINEYARDS fringing the Atlantic and sweeping up toward the craggily peaked mountains behind Cape Town often proclaim them among the world's most spectacular. Do the wines do justice to the majesty of the scenery? Or is there an elevated aura lent by vinous origins steeped in stormy colonial history and in the unique, elaborately gabled Cape-Dutch homesteads and wineries? Or is fascination added by the extraordinary abundance in the variety of wines?

Apartheid politics put the brakes on wine development in South Africa until the early 1990s, when it awoke in a frenzy. Now every imaginable style is made here, from 'port', 'sherry' and brandy, to champagne-method sparkling bruts and botrytis dessert wines, to all the modern classics and a few more, including the Cape's own red, the sometimes sweet, banana-flavoured hybrid, Pinotage. Only lately has it shown occasional glimpses of real quality to raise it from curiosity status.

▽ *Looking across Fairview Estate's vineyards in Paarl to the Simonsberg, an area of high temperatures and low rainfall.*

A few growers even contrive to produce most of these wine types (except 'sherry') on one property, a scatter-gun approach alien to the climate and site-specific ideas espoused in the appellation contrôlée-ruled countries of the Old World. It underlines the fact that South Africa is still in its formative years when it comes to determining suitable pairings between grape varieties and the most compatible terroirs.

Perhaps there is also a lingering novelty value to Cape wine among the world's wine drinkers, after the decades of anti-apartheid isolation. Exports soared – by more than 1,000 per cent in volume to 10 million cases, reaching 50 countries – in the five years after Nelson Mandela removed the taint of Cape wine in politically sensitive markets. Mandela himself, though only an occasional sipper of wine, is a potent national marketing icon.

But the honeymoon could not last forever and it did not take long for a few serious criticisms to surface among the generally polite, sometimes trade-sponsored

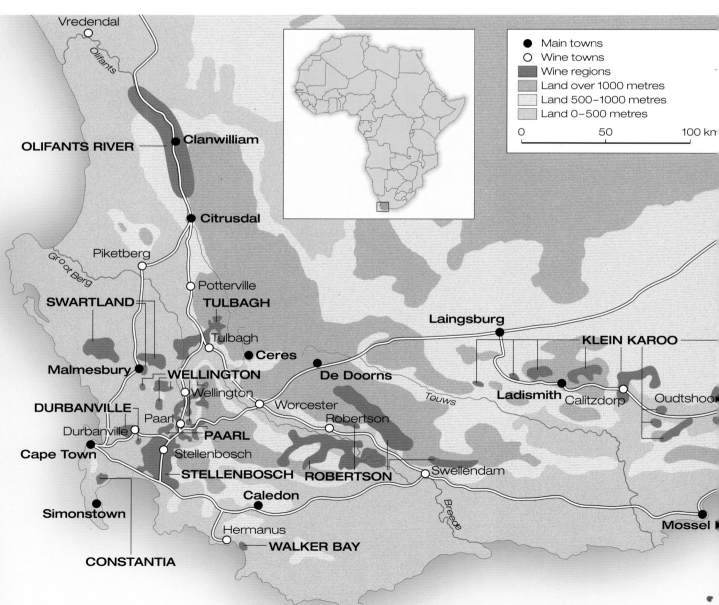

gushings. 'Hard, tannic, unripe reds; flabby dry whites,' were among the negative remarks from a number of the world's most respected palates, comparing the Cape unfavourably with New World competitors. Sensitive nerves were struck in the Cape wine community. South Africa's wine-growers are inured to international ostracism, and reaction from one of the Cape's best-known winemakers, ex-Springbok rugby player Jan Coetzee of Vriesenhof in Stellenbosch, was not untypical. 'I don't give a shit what anybody thinks about my wines ... I like them and think they are damned good. I am not going to change my style for anyone,' he said.

Others responded differently, and headed off on foreign travels to investigate, or to invite expert guidance. Foreign consultants, once rare, are now much more common in South Africa, and are spreading valuable advice. Wine styles are also changing to meet the demands for supermarket-friendly wines, despite a minority of winemakers intent on protecting what they regard as a distinctive Cape wine heritage. The temptations of international recognition, and hard-currency earnings, are modernising and softening styles among the majority of the 4,000 Cape labels on offer, emphasising fruit quality over lean inaccessibility and unripe, terse, tannic bite.

The industry, still small by world standards with 3.4 per cent of global production and an annual harvest of just over one million tonnes, has not forgotten that it was plunging towards bankruptcy before the post-apartheid lift-off in international trade mopped up chronic annual surpluses. Local consumption at under nine litres per capita a year has remained obstinately static; South Africans are mainly beer drinkers.

South Africa may be one of the oldest New World wine regions – wine was first pressed in 1659 by the colonial governor, Jan van Riebeek – but classically made, modern French barrel-aged Cabernet Sauvignons have only been bottled since the mid-1980s. Barrel-fermented Chardonnays are even more recent; it is virtually impossible to buy Cape Chardonnays confidently for five-year bottle-improvement.

Cape growers are still overcoming two blighting legacies, one viticultural, the other political. The crippling leaf roll virus in vineyards, severely inhibiting ripeness, was widespread until just a few years ago – which means that many of the Cape's finer wines are of recent vintages, from relatively young, virus-free vineyards.

And, as late as 1992, vineyard plantings were restricted by the arbitrary and bizarre (from a quality viewpoint) production quotas, which favoured hot-climate, bulk-producing regions. These were imposed by the KWV (Co-operative Grape Growers' Association), a body with statutory powers, representing the 4,500 growers that supply some 71 KWV-affiliated cooperatives, basing their plantings on the country's big brandy industry. As a result, only 17 per cent of the 103,000 hectares of vineyards are planted with the best-selling varietals in modern markets: Cabernet Sauvignon, Merlot, Shiraz, Chardonnay, Sauvignon Blanc and Riesling.

This explains why most of the fine flagship wines of international quality come from new vineyards and wineries, and often from those taking advantage of cool, coastal regions such as Constantia, Walker Bay, Elgin, Somerset West and Darling.

Cape wine has woken from the slumbers of its apartheid isolation. Dated viticulture masquerading as tradition is under scrutiny almost everywhere. And the best is doubtless yet to come.

△ *The traditionally-styled homestead of Buitenverwachting, surrounded by vineyards.*

Stellenbosch

Stellenbosch is the Cape's Napa Valley, a setting for the densest concentration of the country's best-known wine names, both established and recent. It is also the seat of the government's Oenological and Viticultural Research Institute (OVRI) and the official wine quality control body, the Wine and Spirit Board.

Like Napa, recent developments, generated by an influx of newcomers and foreign investment, are lending an air of excitement and showbiz to the Cape wine scene, inflating land prices, driving technological innovation and challenging conventions of all kinds, including old labelling (many featured slave bells) and even some almost sacred architectural fashions.

But tradition and continuity are also emphasised by the headquarters here of the country's two largest wholesaling wine and spirit merchants, Stellenbosch Farmers Winery (SFW) and Distillers Corporation, owned by the Rupert family, the wealthiest in the Cape.

All this confident local power is set in and around the oak-lined university town of Stellenbosch on the Eerste River (First River) with many fine examples of classic, white-gabled Cape Dutch architecture. Stellenbosch was founded in 1679 and is South Africa's second oldest town after Cape Town, a 40-minute drive away on a network of wine routes which also reach into the spectacularly craggy mountain ranges around the town. During summer and autumn sunsets, they can change colours in minutes, from hazy greys and blues to streaked mauves and pinks, making a fantasy world of the winelands.

There's a predictably settled air among these wineries which are now increasingly inundated by hordes of visitors. Many are well-developed, with eating as well as wine tasting facilities, and peak visiting periods are the warm spring and summer months (roughly November to April). The largest establishments, like Blaauwklippen, Delheim and Simonsig, offer an A to Z fruit-salad of wines, including many varietal and blended reds ranging from heavy to light (the most important varietals being Cabernet Sauvignon, Shiraz, Pinot Noir, Merlot, Pinotage), and

whites, both dry and sweet. Sparkling and fortified wines can also be found. Restaurants in this region have multiplied from the early 1990s and the area has sprouted scores of bed and breakfast establishments to meet an acute seasonal accommodation shortage.

Stellenbosch is most often associated with the Cape's finer red wines but this is now a dated tag, misleading on two counts. First, the implied suggestion that lesser Cape reds only hail from beyond Stellenbosch has been laid to rest by convincing latter-day challenges from Constantia, Paarl and Franschhoek. Second, the region does not confine itself to reds; it produces a number of first-class dry whites, including Chardonnay and Sauvignon Blanc, the latter usually said to show best in cool maritime conditions. Though the town itself is tucked away, it is only a 15-minute drive from the coast, and Stellenbosch's viticultural boundaries extend down to False Bay on the Atlantic, where onshore cooling breezes blow daily, especially over the Helderberg mountain range, home to the most elevated and maritime vineyards and the region's most promising viticultural area.

To categorise Stellenbosch climatically or classify its soils is a complex exercise. Too many exceptions exist to the generalisations that the mountainside vineyards are planted on acid, decomposed granite and that the valleys consist of alluvial soils on clay bases. Scientists say there are some 50 soil types and the differently angled slopes and foothills offer a bewildering variety of terroirs, from very hot to sea- or mountain-moderated. Though many vineyards are irrigated (but less so than hotter inland regions) Stellenbosch yields are substantially lower (about 7 tonnes per hectare for reds) than those in the interior. Most soils need heavy lime adjustments, especially before re-planting, to achieve higher pH levels.

The famous, established red wine estates of Meerlust, Kanonkop, Rust-en-Vrede, Uitkyk, Overgaauw, Rustenberg (the last making wine uninterruptedly for more than a century) specialise mainly in Cabernet or Bordeaux-style blends. But their lead has been disputed increasingly in the past decade by new Cape stars, many within Stellenbosch but also beyond.

△ *The Thelema Mountains provide a spectacular backdrop to the vineyards of Stellenbosch.*

The most prized Stellenbosch new wave wines are produced not only from recently-established vineyards (older vines suffered from widespread leaf roll virus infections) but often by winemakers who are newcomers to Cape wine. Thelema Mountain Vineyards' California-trained winemaker Gyles Webb, a former accountant, bottles the most consistently award-winning wines from vineyards which replaced orchards only in the mid-1980s. Thelema was the first winery in the area actively to hire regular international (US) viticultural advice and the benefits are obvious.

Stellenbosch has opened itself up to other ways of improving its wines: new pre-occupations with canopy management to achieve more intense fruit, and controlled yields from vines pruned to achieve balance between foliage and fruit, follow the equally recent but now rapid improvements in clonal vine and rootstock selection. Wholesale changes in vinification and the use of French oak barrels – widely used only since the mid-1980s have also improved quality.

The Stellenbosch gloss is tempered by official industry statistics. The most widely planted variety is Chenin Blanc (accounting for about 28 per cent of the vineyard, mirroring the national average). Chardonnay and Sauvignon Blanc together account for less than 20 per cent of all plantings and the region's speciality, the local red Pinotage grape (a 1926 crossing of Pinot Noir and Cinsault) amounts to no more than seven per cent of the vineyard area, which in total comprises no more than 15 per cent of the country's total 103,000 hectares.

Constantia

A determined 1990s wine revival is in progress in Cape Town's southwestern suburbs, where former glories are being reclaimed in the oldest vineyard region of the Cape, and the site of the first and still most famous South African wine farm, Groot Constantia.

This government-run estate, and the nearby privately-owned wineries and vineyards, were neglected for most of this century, and last. But viticulturalists are unanimous in believing this thin, southern peninsula poking into the southern

Atlantic, with its pronounced exposure to maritime and mountain influences, is ideal for quality wine. Vineyards of similar varieties elsewhere often ripen two or three weeks earlier; the longer ripening time, combined with sea-breezy days, is another contributor to finesse and intensity.

Most of the soils in Constantia are water-retentive, clay-rich, decomposing granites and loamy sandstones which do not require supplementary irrigation; natural rainfall exceeds 1,000 millimetres annually anyway. Average temperatures at 18-19°C are among the lowest of any Cape wine region.

Colonial society's hedonistic heyday was recorded here in the earliest grand examples of Cape Dutch homesteads and in the early 1800s Constantia wine. This was the powerful, unctuous Muscat de Frontignac-based red and white dessert wines that yielded to none except Hungarian Tokaji in popularity and expense at European courts. It was not even upstaged by grand Bordeaux, yet to establish its 1855 classifications at this point.

But the vagaries of colonial and European wars and eventual removal of preferential tariffs, not to mention phylloxera in the 1870s and domestic wine gluts in the early 20th century (which swung production in favour of bulk brandy grape varieties) all played a part in Constantia's vinous eclipse as Cape Town expanded and most farming land yielded to urban sprawl.

Convincing proof, however, of modern wine quality has been bottled since the mid-1980s, when Klein Constantia (adjoining Groot Constantia) was re-developed with new-clone, virus-free vineyards by its new owner, Duggie Jooste and his winemaker, Ross Gower, a South African trained in Germany and New Zealand.

Fine, piercing, big Cape benchmark Sauvignon Blancs, with subtle vintage variations, have been bottled since 1986. Impressive Cabernets and rich Chardonnays – Gower believes in wines with impact – are also grown at this thoroughly New World, technologically sophisticated estate. And, with its Vin de Constance, Klein Constantia is reviving the old Constantia dessert wine traditions, with precisely the same Muscat clones and vinification methods used centuries ago. Grape bunch stems

△ *The vineyards of the Klein Constantia Estate have been redeveloped with new, virus-free vine clones.*

are twisted when ripe and then left on the vine. This allows them to shrivel into raisins which when pressed, yield concentrated juice with high levels of alcohol, almost botrytis-like nuances and great complexity.

Next door and also among the leafy suburbs is Buitenverwachting (in Afrikaans 'beyond expectation'), a 1980s German investment that has spared no expense in vineyard renewal of modern classic varieties and in cellar technology. It has produced perhaps the most polished all-round Cape revivalist wine performance to date, with exceptional Cabernets, Chardonnays, Sauvignon Blancs and Rieslings. Like Klein Constantia, Buitenverwachting's immaculate new cellars blend in with the more traditional architecture of the homesteads. It is an excellent winery to visit, not least because it is home to one of South Africa's finest restaurants; most surveys place it in the top three or four. You may also catch a glimpse of the baboons which regularly invaded all Constantia vineyards fringing the upper slopes by scaling the fences, a sharp annual barometer of approaching ripeness in the grapes. Vineyard workers banging tins frighten off the marauders.

Steenberg is the latest large, and also ultra-quality-conscious, wine development, established around an 18-hole golf course and retirement complex, complete with restaurant. A promising, crisp first Sauvignon was produced here in 1995.

These successes have spurred the fabled old estate Groot Constantia itself – among Cape Town's most visited tourist attractions – to look to its laurels. Beginning, in 1989, with a complete rethink on vineyard-varietal site compatibility, the winemaker, Martin Moore, has begun to offer modern, balanced wines. A Bordeaux-styled Cabernet and Merlot blend, named Gouverneurs Reserve, is a top-of-the-range, new-oaked and well regarded label. However, Moore is also compelled to bottle a wide selection of wines, including semi-sweets, mainly from Chenin Blanc, and rosés, to pacify the swarms of sweeter-toothed local holiday visitors from South Africa's northern provinces.

Durbanville

Suburbia has steadily fanned out from Cape Town, in this instance northwest, steadily swallowing up Durbanville's remaining farmland. But a few vineyards have held fast, and experts agree they are privileged sites, constantly brushed by the southern Atlantic less than ten 15 kilometres away. Not only do the breezes moderate the African sunshine – to a low daily average 19°C during the growing season – they aerate the vineyards and minimise fungal diseases.

The Parkers at Altydgedacht are long-established vignerons, who have experimented with all kinds of varieties in their suburbia-surrounded vineyards, including the country's only Barbera, the Italian red grape, and Gamay. Their rendering of Pinotage, much less aggressive than the national average and barrel-aged in American oak, is well regarded, as is a super-flowery Gewürztraminer. Good Cabernets, grown in the generally deep, red decomposed granite soils that can nurse vine roots through hot summers, are made by Diemersdal, an estate with 300 years of wine growing to its name, and Bloemendal, the latter also producing a dry, refreshing bottle-fermented sparkling wine.

Walker Bay

Historically there was never much viticulture in this coastal region but even the little that did exist seems to have been abandoned decades ago. On the hour-long coastal drive east from Cape Town to Hermanus, the main seaside town and smart holiday resort in the bay, visitors pass orchards, then rolling wheat fields and sheep farms. There's barely a vine to be seen.

But for many close watchers of developing trends, this cool ocean climate region is among South Africa's most promising. It has only seven – all young – winemaking establishments, but several more are on the drawing board.

There would still probably be none but for the pioneering Tim Hamilton Russell, a loner in some ways and, back in 1978, still a Johannesburg-based J Walter Thompson advertising chief executive. He tentatively planted a few Cabernet vines on the windy hills behind the family holiday cottage at Hermanus … and has not looked back since. At the time he was well adrift – physically and philosophically – of mainstream South African growers. And he was actively discouraged by the wine production controlling body at the KWV headquarters, which has always preferred conformism. The soils, sandy and shale mostly, were generally shallow and uninviting, despite some deeper pockets gravel and clay. The strong off-shore winds were sometimes vine-threatening. The Cabernet vines were also hard of ripening. Walker Bay, by Cape standards, is cool, rivalling Constantia with growing season average daily temperatures of under 20°C.

Undaunted – encouraged even that he'd hit upon good Burgundy aspects – Hamilton Russell planted Pinot Noir and Chardonnay and by 1985 his reputation in both had been secured. Another South African viticultural region had been discovered. More importantly, others were encouraged to explore beyond traditional safe sites and challenge KWV-inspired shibboleths. Now Hamilton Russell's Oxford-educated son, Anthony, an equally persuasive marketer, has taken over and begun expanding the business. He's trying Pinotage, for example, and the first (1995) bottling shows the same careful handling in oak as current winemaker Kevin Grant displays with the winery's Pinot Noirs; a regional understated delicacy is evident.

The early Pinot Noir vineyards, planted with the only clone available at the time, a Swiss one known locally as BK5, are being phased out; virus-debilitated like all Cape Pinot vineyards of the same Pinot clone, they produced wines which tended to brown prematurely. The first vintages with significant proportions of new, more brightly tinted Burgundy clones, show firmer colours. Hamilton Russell Jnr, however, is keen to preserve some of the understated, organic and traditional Burgundian smells and flavours which characterised earlier vintages and which he believes are in any event the outcome of his vineyard terroir.

The Hamilton Russell winery's former Burgundy-wise winemaker, Peter Finlayson, was the first to repeat the exercise, establishing Pinot Noir, Chardonnay and Sauvignon Blanc on the slopes next door, this time with French involvement. Then one of the Cape's few women winemakers, Storm Kreusch-Dau (who was also a Hamilton Russell winemaker formerly) set up the WhaleHaven winery, using the same grape varietals.

△ Father and son team, Tim and Anthony Hamilton Russell have exploited the cool climate potential of Walker Bay.

Peter Finlayson is less complicated in his Pinot Noir aims than Hamilton Russell – and anyway strives for a more hard-hitting, initially more tannic version of burgundy, which he too believes is an honest reflection of his terroir. He planted new Pinot Noir clones at the outset and trellised in a variety of ways, including an adaptation of the French Guyot pruning system and dense plantings.

Further inland at Bot River, growers previously shipping to cooperatives, have begun labelling their own wines, most promising among them the Beaumont Pinotages and the Wildekrans Sauvignon Blancs. These are widely scattered vineyards but they form a link with the higher, wooded and frequently mist-covered Elgin area – and the country's finest apple-growing farms. Financial rewards have always been vastly higher for fruit exports than vine growing. A handful of these Elgin apple growers have, however, been persuaded to experiment with vineyards and the results have startled the traditionalists. Paul Cluver is the best-known name and in 1997 inaugurated the area's first winery (previously selling grapes to Nederburg in Paarl).

Franschhoek

The name means 'French Corner' in Afrikaans because many of the Cape-bound French Huguenot refugees settled here in 1688. The valley was also called Olifantshoek because elephants roamed among the beautiful hills and streams, dominated by a majestic amphitheatre of mountains.

The elephants and the French language have long since disappeared – though many of the vineyard names – La Motte, L'Ormarins, Clos Cabrière and Chamonix, for example – echo the French ties. But there might be a case for a name change now – Engelse Hoek or 'English Corner'. The valley has been colonised in the past decade by English-speaking growers intent on breathing new viticultural life into the region and ridding its past reputation for bulk, cooperative quality wine only; one large facility, the Franschhoek Cooperative, once handled the grapes of some 120 farmer members, many of them more pre-occupied with fruit and vegetables.

That has all changed. Nearly a dozen small wineries have been built and more are planned – there are scores of new, avant-garde labels and producers who don't have their own wineries and are contracting the vinification of grapes for their own labels. Restaurants have multiplied tenfold in the past five years and the once sleepy village with its gracious little museum dedicated to those early European pioneers is now among the busiest of all destinations in the winelands.

The most important viticulturally has been in varietal shift, mainly from an indifferent clone of Sémillon. Many vineyards were untrellised, planted one metre by one metre, the rows too narrow to be worked by anything except horses. Dense planting may yet return, but in the meantime more conventional two to three metre spacing is practised as the vineyards have been planted to the popular varieties of Chardonnnay, Sauvignon Blanc, new clones of Sémillon and Riesling. Chenin Blanc is still popular and fine, conventionally oak-aged reds are appearing.

And from none more so than the valley's liveliest bon vivant and more serious innovator, Achim von Arnim. He arrived in the valley in 1981 and by 1985 was producing Franschhoek's first *méthode champenoise* sparkling wine at Clos Cabrière, from bought-in Chardonnay and Pinot Noir. He expanded up from the valley floor to more gravelly, clay-rich soils and in 1994 produced what was widely acclaimed as a breakthrough South African Pinot Noir – supple and soft, with cherry and spice flavours.

La Motte, a modern winery with a French quality-conscious winemaker Jacques Borman, has been bottling outstanding Shiraz and Cabernet since the late 1980s. L'Ormarins, with equally impressive facilities and a grand homestead, has wines of weight and class – and a wider spread of varietal choice. All these producers and others belong to the Vignerons de Franschhoek, an association which has established a wine route and offering tastings at some of the most scenically situated farms, along the Berg river and up in the hills.

New investment and expansion in the 1990s have set new challenges for Franschhoek and the current state of flux promises much experiment before definitive patterns of quality and viticultural strengths are stabilised.

△ *Elephants once roamed through the Franschhoek area which was originally settled by French Huguenots.*

Paarl

Stellenbosch, only about 30 kilometres south towards the ocean, may present the glamorous face of Cape wine but Paarl is the seat of real power. In 1917 the giant Co-operative Growers' Association, the KWV, was formed here, uniting all wine farmers under a single banner. Since then the government has granted the massive and influential organisation extensive policing powers to limit wine production by quotas and to fix prices.

Until they were progressively dismantled from the early 1990s, these privileges cushioned the lives of some 4,500 member farmers, all but about 150 (who made their own wines) delivering grapes to a network of 71 KWV-affiliated cooperatives spread throughout the Cape winelands. The KWV mopped up surpluses and, at its own sprawling 18-hectare facilities in Paarl, converted these into various by-products and industrial alcohols. It also made a wide range of 'sherries and 'ports' and a full range of well-priced table wines for export under its own labels.

Since anti-apartheid sanctions were lifted and exports soared, buyers have been beating a path to the KWV's Cape-Georgian Paarl headquarters, La Concorde. Vineyards creep up to the town's main street – and across from La Concorde, the organisation's own showcase estate, La Borie, is open to visitors for tastings while a restaurant offers Cape fare.

Paarl – meaning 'pearl' in Afrikaans because the giant, rounded rocks overlooking the town glisten after rain – is regarded as a warm region although the mountain ranges sweeping down to the valleys and the Berg River winding west provide many farms with moderating aspects.

A fair generalisation, though, is that Paarl wines are broader and heavier than coastal counterparts. The same mixed approach to vine varieties prevalent elsewhere applies to Paarl too, and big establishments such as Nederburg (700,000 cases a year) Backsberg, Villiera, Fairview and Landskroon, and ultra-large cooperatives like Simonsvlei, source their own or grower-supplier grapes from a spread of soils and micro-climates.

Poorer, relatively porous, sandy Table Mountain sandstones are a valley floor feature and vineyards there, with shallow root penetration, need frequent irrigation in summer when temperatures reaching into the high 30°Cs are common. In the northern reaches of Paarl, beyond Wellington and toward Tulbagh, shale becomes more frequent and the same distinctive pattern of acidic, weathered granite can be found on the mountains.

Though the region, with lower natural rainfalls than the coast (often less than 400 millimetres a year), does not boast the buzz and spread of activity in Stellenbosch, the technological and viticultural revolution has not passed by here.

In fact, a handful of both new and old wine names are among the most ground-breaking. At Fairview on the southwest side of Paarl Rock, the experimental Charles Back is one of the Cape's best-travelled and most adventurous winemakers, who incorporates Australian and adapted French *maceration carbonique* production ideas to maximise fruity approachability in many of his long list of wine types. Particularly popular are his Shiraz, Pinotage, Chardonnay (all well-oaked) and Chenin Blancs of all styles, plus rosés and a Gamay. He is the first Cape grower to bottle a commercial Viognier.

At the ultra-chic, re-modelled Plaisir de Merle on the east-facing slopes of the Simonsberg, Stellenbosch Farmers' Winery (SFW) has used Château Margaux's Paul Pontallier as a consultant to produce a maiden 1993 Cabernet that is showing a new Cape capacity for ripe-tannined accessibility. And Napa's Donald Hess (of The Hess Collection) was so impressed by Glen Carlou's Chardonnays that he bought into the 20,000-case a year winery in 1996.

On the hotter, northwestern side of Paarl, South Africa's top international tenor, Zurich-based Deon van der Walt, has invested in a new winery, Veenwouden which produces a range of internationally-acclaimed wines. Van der Walt's winemaker brother Marcel uses the services of the celebrated French oenologist, Michel Rolland, whose influence is reflected in the estate's fine Bordeaux-blend – which contradicts the idea that warm-area fruit only makes hot, coarse wine.

△ *The mountains of Paarl are said to gleam like pearls in the rain and gave the district its Afrikaans name.*

Wellington

The majority of the Cape vine nurseries have congregated in these warm valleys between Paarl and Tulbagh, and there's a mixed-farming feel to the town and its surrounds; sheep graze in paddocks, guavas are a much-planted fruit, wheatlands stretch west beyond the nurseries. But among the wooded northeastern foothills of the impressive mountains around the historic Bains Pass – for long the Cape's main gateway north – a few recent bottlings have provided interest, beyond the cheerful everyday wines offered by the local cooperatives.

Swartland

The Swartland ('blackland') is the open, rolling, large-scale wheatland area, stretching westwards from Cape Town, and is a complete contrast to the picturesque mountainous landscapes in the Cape capital's immediate hinterland. It is an unlikely looking vineyard region – and marginal in its low rainfall, with only 250 millimetres a year on average. But looks are deceptive. Several sites near Swartland's coast – notably around Darling (to which thousands of foreign visitors flock for the stunning wild flowers that carpet the flat lands to the horizon in spring) – and the occasional high, cool outcrops rising off the undulating plains offer friendlier viticultural conditions, albeit on widely scattered and small scales at Piketberg, Porterville and Riebeek West.

In fact Darling, and the other west coast area around Saldhana as well as the interior mountain sites, are now more frequently mentioned as potential sources of new and distinctive grape quality in the future. Until 1991, official production quotas limited private exploration in these regions. The generally cooler west coast, brushed by the Benguela current from the Antarctic, is hampered chiefly by a lack of water except in those mountain spots where rainfall can be trapped by dams and along the rare streams.

The dusty, unremarkable town of Malmesbury is the centre of Swartland and the location of one of the Cape's big cooperatives, Swartland Wine Cellar. Its chief

winemaker, Johan de Villiers, says the lack of irrigation and predominantly thinner, shale soils (with granite and sandstone patches elsewhere) act as a natural brake on over-production, with yields commonly under eight tonnes per hectare for the commonest, and altogether most ubiquitous variety in the Cape, Chenin Blanc, here called Steen. Swartland Steen can be racily fresh and aromatic, though short-lived. Good Sauvignon Blancs are also a feature and de Villiers produces hearty, softish, unfussy reds from Pinotage and Shiraz.

Darling vineyards have yielded exceptionally crisp, gooseberry-tasting Sauvignon Blancs for a Stellenbosch winemaker, Neil Ellis, who is adept at sourcing characterful, regional fruit; he was first to buy in Sauvignon Blanc in the mid-1980s when the apple area of Elgin was still considered off-limits to grapes.

Though Swartland follows the general South African tendency toward producing more than two-thirds white wine, one of the country's consistently good 'port' styles comes from the Allesverloren Estate at Riebeck West, owned by the Malan family. A late-bottled version, made mostly from Souzão and Tinta Barocca grapes, is produced in conditions as trying and hot as the Douro Valley in Portugal.

Tulbagh

The notion that fine, bottle-fermented sparkling wine, produced by what is termed Method Cap Classique in South Africa, might hail from the distant heat bowl around the mountain-fringed hamlet of Tulbagh would seem far-fetched on paper. However, at the 274-hectare, 200-year-old Krone family estate at Twee Jonge Gezellen, just north of the town, they've been producing a fresh, racy bubbly since 1987 from Chardonnay and Pinot Noir. The estate's owner, Nicky Krone, became the first South African to strike a partnership with a Champagne House – Mumm – in 1995, bottling a Brut closely styled on the estate's own Krone Borealis.

As with the handful of other producers in the valley, the emphasis here is on white varieties, the majority of vineyard planted to Muscats (de Frontignac and d'Alexandrie). However Sémillon and Riesling are also grown. Some 15 varieties are

△ *Mountains surround the hot vineyards of Tulbagh where the grape varieties are harvested at night to avoid the heat.*

planted at Twee Jonge Gezellen by Krone, an inveterate tinkerer who pioneered night time harvesting in South Africa and whose father was among the developers of the then revolutionary cold-fermentation in the 1960s, foreshadowing the advance from traditional, oxidised sweet wines.

Stony, gravelly soils on a clay base are common here until the vineyards ascend the hillsides where they change to decomposed granites; but growers owe their good fortune to the high Sarelberg in the west, which provides early afternoon respite from the summer heat.

Worcester

'On the other side of the mountain,' say coastal people, just a touch dismissively, when they talk of the Worcester region, until recently only accessible by the arduous Du Toits Kloof pass north of Paarl, now rapidly through a tunnel. But a vast network of private wineries (very few registered estates) and large cooperatives account for a quarter of South Africa's wine production.

Less tourist-conscious than along the coastal belt, the growth of private labels and wineries has been slower – and is reflected in the choice of grape varieties. More than 70 per cent of all vineyards are devoted to *vin ordinaire* white grapes including Chenin Blanc, Colombard, Palomino and Hanepoot (Muscat d'Alexandrie). Until 1996, Chardonnay accounted for only 4.2 per cent of vineyards.

Like the Robertson region further east, Worcester's generally drier farms are dependent on the nearby Brandvlei dam as the Antarctic weather systems deposit most of their valuable rain nearer the seaboard. Beyond the lee of the Worcester mountains, annual rainfall can be a paltry 200 millimetres. The mountains are occasionally snow-capped in winter – and some promotional literature has used the snowy pictures, just a little self-consciously, to try and counter a supposed hot-climate stigma. To the far north of the area at De Doorns, table grape farming is the main activity.

A number of the leading cooperatives – Du Doitskloof, De Wet and Nuy especially – have made outstanding dry whites. Most of the wineries are good at producing simple, fruity Colombards and Chenin Blancs, mainly in the semi-sweet styles preferred by the majority of South Africans. But the region is also one of the main suppliers of luscious fortified Muscats (for which there is a dwindling market) and of bulk blending wines.

This is changing. The area is fertile, with plenty of loamy and alluvial, stony soils, and the close concentration of big wineries with modern stainless steel, good cooling equipment and one of the biggest bottling facilities in South Africa, has attracted foreign supermarket buyers who now see Worcester as a bargain source of well-made wines for immediate drinking.

Robertson

This Scottish-sounding but very Afrikaans-speaking semi-desert inland region owes its existence as a wine and brandy producing area to a single lifeline – the slow-flowing Breede River (Broad River) and the Brandvlei Dam upstream near Worcester.

The Breede runs eastwards into the Indian Ocean, for a while paralleling the shimmering Langeberge Mountains to the north which fringe the sleepy, tin-roofed town of Robertson on the valley floor.

Before the Brandvlei Dam was built at the turn of the century the river often ran dry in the summer and the hearty, polite and close-knit Dutch- and Huguenot-descended farmers usually made their living from other agricultural pursuits including sheep-rearing. Many still raise what is the centrepiece of the cuisine here – Karoo lamb, spit-roasted and dripping with singed fat, served with hearty mounds of sweetened pumpkin.

But they make, and drink, mainly white wines. Among the region's vinous specialities are fortified Muscats, both red and white, often deliciously full at about 17-18 per cent alcohol, very sweet and spicily aromatic. Muscat d'Alexandrie – locally called Hanepoot – is the lowlier white but the finer-berried Muscadels (spelt variously Muskadel and Muscadelle), are made from Muscat de Frontignan, believed to be among the original grape vines brought to South Africa more than three centuries ago by the first colonial Dutch Governor, Jan van Riebeeck.

Two natural features favour the future of Robertson wine quality in modern export markets: the frequent outcrops of calcium-rich soils so rare in the Cape, and the cold night time temperatures which lower the average readings, to just over 22°C during spring and summer, when daytime 35°C days are common, and slow down what otherwise would be a searing and rapid ripening of grapes with resulting loss of fruit quality.

Robertson and its neighbouring (and also British-sounding) villages – Ashton, McGregor, Bonnievale, Montagu – can be approached either from Worcester in the west or from the eastern towns near the southern ocean, Caledon or Swellendam. Either way, the visitor drives on broad, open roads and encounters expansive, rolling countryside mostly covered in grey, knee-height scrub (and wheatlands toward the coast) stretching away into the mountains from a patchwork of vineyards.

From among these, wineries loom out, some no-nonsense, sprawling cooperatives processing 20-30,000 tonnes of grapes a year in echoing corridors of big, stainless steel and cement tanks; one is a futuristic curved, multi-coloured, purple and orange structure. More conservative plain white and thatch Cape Dutch or clean-lined Georgian facades belong to independent traditionalists, usually surrounded by gardens of bright-coloured red and white bougainvillaea, roses and cannas.

The Robertson Wine Trust was formed in the early 1990s to organise the 31 wineries into a cohesive marketing body, with maps and information brochures. Like most areas of the Cape, bed and breakfast establishments have mushroomed in the 1990s, from an array of French and Dutch names showing Old World roots in Cape wine – Mon Don, Bon Courage, Clairvaux, Jonkheer, Mooiuitsig.

The more lucrative classic white grape varieties – Chardonnay, Sauvignon Blanc, Riesling and Gewürztraminer – began supplanting the workhorse varieties of Chenin Blanc and Colombard as recently as the early 1980s. However the last two still account for more than half of the region's 11-12,000-hectare plantings – about ten per cent of South Africa's total. Though useful as brandy base, Robertson Chenin

△ *The workhorse varieties of Chenin Blanc and Colombard dominate the semi-desert region of Robertson.*

Blanc and Colombard can also produce excellent but short-lived, reasonably-priced fruity, guava-scented dry and off-dry whites.

Lately, a few Chardonnay-based sparkling wines have been made, and well-praised at international showings, notably by a newcomer to the area, Graham Beck, a coal-mining magnate who bought his Madeba property just outside Robertson, initially to rear a racing stud. The area's calcium soils are as useful to the bone-formation of pedigreed horseflesh as they are to vines.

Growers are also beginning to challenge the long-held belief that the region is too warm and too water-dependent to produce concentrated, fine reds.

Now others are starting to plant Cabernet, Pinot Noir (some for sparkling wine) and Merlot with higher planting densities, canopy methods and reduced yields, determined to bottle wines of a much higher quality than before.

The best-known wineries (and with good visitor tasting facilities) are Graham Beck, Springfield, Zandvliet, Weltevrede, De Wetshof, Bon Courage, Van Loveren. Many establishments continue to offer a varietal and stylistic spread, from heavy dessert wines, including 'port' and the Muscats, to semi-sweet whites, to dry classics such as Chardonnay and the occasional red. The best-known cooperatives are Rooiberg, Robertson, McGregor, Ashton, Roodezandt and Bonnievale.

Klein Karoo

By the time travellers reach this hot, dry, semi-desert region – about four hours' drive north east from Cape Town – ostrich and sheep-rearing are the more obvious and visible farming options. The imposing mountain ranges fringing the coast yield to more undulating and sparser ridges. But then, around towns like Outshoorn and Calitzdorp, with help from the river beds and dams storing winter water, a few wine growers (contributing only 3.5 per cent of South Africa's production) coax life from vineyards. In fact, the combination of deep alluvial river-bank soils, irrigation and very dry, high temperatures can make for prolific yields. The national grape variety pattern is repeated here, ie predominantly white, mostly (25 per cent) Chenin Blanc;

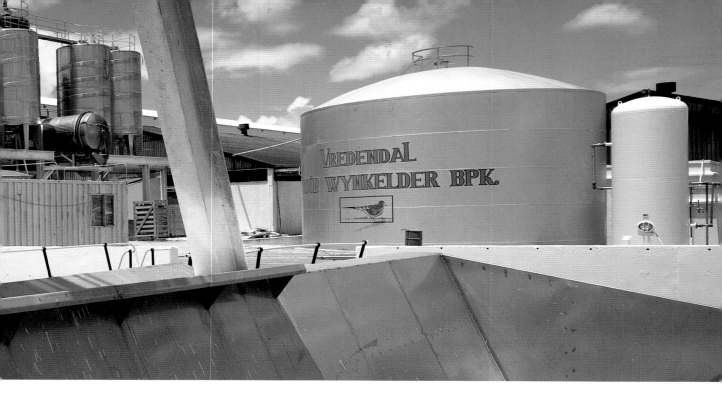

brandy grapes Colombard and Palomino also feature strongly and prized fortified Muscadels are produced.

But Calitzdorp is perhaps best-known as the 'port' capital of South Africa, largely due to the energy of the long-established Nel family there, on the Boplaas and Die Krans estates. They were among the first Cape producers in the late 1980s to plant the 'Rolls-Royce' of Portuguese port varieties, Touriga Nacional. This now joins the more prevalent Tinta Barocca and occasional Souzão port vines. Boplaas' Carel Nel has also been pursuing his idea of growing the conventional classics of Sauvignon Blanc, Riesling and Chardonnay at the eastern extremities of traditional winelands, near Mossel Bay, but so far with limited success. These vineyards fringe summer rainfall regions but are cooler than at inland Calitzdorp.

Olifants River

The baking summer heat around the Olifants River make this a bulk wine and table grape haven, although its winters are generally milder. The equivalent latitude in the northern hemisphere would place the Olifants River region well into Morocco – nearby Paarl is at a similar latitude (33.4 degrees) in the southern hemisphere as Jerez in Spain is in the northern.

Because of such searing heat conventional and flood irrigation of the fertile red soils and silt by the river is essential for the cultivation of grapes, and results in enormous yields of 30 to 40 tonnes per hectare.

Here you'll find the Vredendal cooperative, South Africa's largest, processing nearly 60,000 tonnes of grapes in 1996. Even buyers from Europe's largest supermarkets have been overcome by the endless rows of gigantic stainless steel tanks – mostly full of sound dry white wine, typically Colombard/Chenin Blanc blends. Occasional stabs have been made at Chardonnay (from a coastal vineyard at Koekenap) and at Ruby Cabernet (a Cabernet Sauvignon-Carignan cross) and a prolific yielder. So, for all these unlikely drawbacks to quality, the region has scored well commercially in export markets with early-season light dry white table wines.

△ *The massive Vredendal cooperative, South Africa's largest, can handle 2,000 tonnes of grapes daily.*

Recommended Producers

Stellenbosch

Thelema Mountain Vineyards – Among the hottest new wave Cape wine names. From high mountain vineyards on Simonsberg, behind Stellenbosch come distinctive, modern-style, sweet-minty and accessible reds: Cabernets, Merlots and blends of both. Emphasis on ripe tannins, supple textures, complex fruit, careful oaking. Consistently delicious fruity Sauvignon Blancs; rich barrel-fermented Chardonnays.

Mulderbosch Vineyards – From a standing start in 1991, now a top South African Sauvignon Blanc producer. Winemaker Dobrovic a fan, after study trips there, of New Zealand Sauvignons Blancs. Also a gently-oaked version (Blanc Fume), a fine, softer Bordeaux-style blend named Faithful Hound and a still-rare dry, oak-aged Chenin Blanc.

Meerlust Estate – Fabled name in Cape wine – after eight generations, still in the Myburgh family – and a survivor against much intensified competition. The Cape's only Italian winemaker, Dalla Cia, veers shy of overtly approachable fruitiness in reds, preferring classic dry. Since 1995, also produce an emphatic Chardonnay, with 16 months in heavily-toasted new oak; plus first estate Grappa.

Warwick Estate – Delicious, complex and uncharacteristically fine Pinotage added since 1995 to Canadian-born Ratcliffe's range of claret-styled reds, including a varietally labelled Cabernet Franc. Top wine is oak-aged Trilogy – Cabernets Franc and Sauvignon with Merlot.

Rustenberg Estate – Completely revamped old estate, famous for its reds made in oak-lined, Cape Dutch setting. Cellar now headed by young New Zealand winemaker with antipodean zest for clean, modern fruity whites and balanced, ripe-tannined Cabernets and Cabernet blends.

Neil Ellis Wines – With no vineyards of his own, from mid-1980s Neil Ellis pioneered Cape outsourcing of grapes from up to 15 widely scattered growers; then selling under his own label. Always interesting, intense Cabernets, often outstanding Sauvignon Blancs and barrel-aged Chardonnays, made at his Jonkershoek Valley cellar in Stellenbosch.

Saxenburg Wines – This Swiss-owned, re-developed property came from nowhere in the 1990s to produce a fine, intensely spicy Cape Shiraz finished in American oak. Since then other wines have been added including Sauvignon Blanc, Chardonnay, Pinotage and, Cabernet Sauvignon. Fruit intensity always a feature; balance and finesse increasingly so.

Stellenzicht Vineyards – Lavishly equipped winery, completely re-planted vineyards. Winemaker Van Rensburg, here since 1993, has shot this label to fame, with a super-fine, deep-flavoured Stellenzicht Syrah (Shiraz), and also a piercing, fresh Sauvignon Blanc. Botrytis dessert wines (Sauvignon and Riesling) from here and sister property Neethlingshof are undisputed national champions.

Jordan Vineyards – American-trained Jordan couple are making world-class Chardonnays and Sauvignon Blancs; good Cabernets too. Another relatively new but well-integrated winery/vineyard operation on high vineyards with fresh maritime exposure.

Vergelegen Wines – Recently revamped historic estate, now with an avant-garde, French-designed winery sunk three floors deep into a hilltop allowing gentle movement of wine by gravity. New vineyards of Merlot, Chardonnay, Sauvignon Blanc now producing outstanding wines. Widely travelled winemaker Meinert stays in touch with good French connections, including Château Lafite.

Bredell Wines – Rich, sumptuous, densely-concentrated 'port' – from Souzão and Tinta Barocca. A Cape benchmark. Grown in poor, sandy-loam soils, with low-yielding untrellised vines facing the False Bay coast.

Yonder Hill Wines – Small, cult winery, with ground-breaking Merlots on miniscule scale, from own Helderberg vineyards near False Bay coast, now receiving more recognition as an sub-area of the Stellenbosch wine region.

Grangehurst – Small-scale winery (3,500 cases) without own vineyards but specialising in red wine and sourcing grapes from Helderberg area. Winemaker Walker coaxes this plush but firm fruit into bottle after careful oak-ageing. The result is some excellent Cabernet Sauvignon and Pinotage.

Zonnebloem – The upmarket, ubiquitous range from large, well-established Stellenbosch Farmers' Winery; unflamboyant but reliable, balanced reds, including Merlot, Shiraz, Pinotage, Cabernet Sauvignon; often fresh dry white wines, including Sauvignon Blanc, and also some good value Chenin Blanc and Colombard blends.

Kanonkop Estate – Big local reputation for Cabernet Sauvignon and Cabernet-based blend, under Paul Sauer label. Also, until recently, acknowledged leading producer of oaky Pinotage, which winemaker Truter also makes on a more commercial scale for nearby sister winery, Beyerskloof, from bought-in Stellenbosch grapes.

Simonsig Estate – Among South Africa's leading all-round wineries, using grapes from the family's own extensive Stellenbosch vineyards; a creditable showing throughout the range of more than 20 labels; particularly popular for Shiraz, Pinotage, Cabernet Sauvignon, Chardonnay and medium-priced semi-sweet dessert wines, including a first-rate Gewürztraminer.

Constantia

Klein Constantia Estate – A South African star since the mid-1980s. Model, modern cellar, drawing on immaculately planned and maintained vineyards, moderated by nearby mountains and ocean. New Zealand-trained Ross Gower turns in impressive, figgy-asparagus flavoured Sauvignon Blancs; a sumptuous dessert wine from Muscat de Frontignac echoes the famed Constantia dessert wines made here in the last century. Lately, a convincing Pinot Noir.

Buitenverwachting Wines – German-owned and, like its neighbour Klein Constantia, a showpiece winery with replanted vineyards from mid-1980s in prime sites; outstanding Cabernet Sauvignon and a Merlot blend named Christine. Always among the top Sauvignon Blancs; penetrating gooseberry, big but balanced. Also produce a delicate Riesling.

Groot Constantia Estate – The original South African showpiece, established in 1680s. Largely left behind in current renaissance (apart from well-regarded Cabernet/Merlot blend, Gouverneurs Reserve) but now showing promise with Sauvignon Blanc and Chardonnay. The rush of tourists to the estate, many unconnected with wine, results in a whole gamut of wine styles. In the past, quality in cellar and vineyard was affected but this is now improving.

Durbanville

Altydgedacht Estate – Noted for South Africa's only Barbera (Italian red grape variety), but also a highly-scented dry white Gewürztraminer and a full, ripe banana-flavoured Pinotage, all made at a tiny rural holdout in Cape Town's northern urban sprawl by the traditionalist Parker family.

Walker Bay

Bouchard-Finlayson Wines – First Cape/French joint venture, albeit on a small scale, negotiated by winemaker Peter Finlayson, an avowed Burgundy admirer. Now receiving general approval for polished, gutsy Chardonnays (from several far-flung vineyards), and more mixed reviews for early bottlings of home-grown new clone Pinot Noirs. They're full-flavoured, quite tannic – big, rather than shy and delicate.

Hamilton Russell Vineyards – During the 1980s this was the first Cape winery and vineyard to show more than a nodding acquaintance with the Burgundian style of production for Chardonnay and Pinot Noir, in the then still-ignored Hermanus area of Walker Bay. Plantings of fruitier Pinot Noir clones are now improving on previous vintages, and the Chardonnay made here has established itself as a South African standard bearer. Also good at Sauvignon Blanc and Pinotage – look for the Southern Right label.

Franschhoek

Cabrière Estate – Since 1984, it has specialised in several extra-dry champagne-method sparkling wines made with Chardonnay and Pinot Noir. From 1994, produced a dramatic Cape improvement using a new clone of Pinot Noir from densely planted vines; the quality confirmed by a supple and well-balanced 1996 wine.

La Motte Estate – From mainly light, sandy, stony soils it produces some fine, spicy Shiraz, and a convincing Bordeaux-blend of Cabernet Sauvignon and Merlot; also a convincing Sauvignon Blanc, one of the few impressive oaked versions of this wine made in the Cape.

Bellingham Wines – A long list of commercial wines obscures a few recent good Sauvignon Blancs, Chardonnays and interesting if unclassical dry white blends –

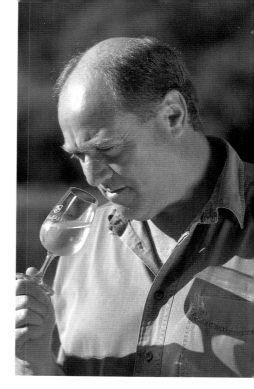

△ Neil Ellis, winemaker for the world's fifth largest winery at Stellenbosch; their brands include Nederburg and Zonnebloem.

Sauvignon Blanc/Chardonnay (Sauvenay) and Cabernet Franc and Shiraz, made by the dedicated young winemaker Charles Hopkins, who is notably receptive to ideas from the New World competition.

L'Ormarins Estate – Rich and generously-barrelled Cabernet Sauvignon/Merlot/Cabernet Franc blend called Optima is among the Cape's best: also powerful Chardonnay and oak-aged Sauvignon, from immaculate mountain-side vineyards and a hi-tech cellar. Ornate visitor tasting rooms.

Boschendal Estate – Produce a good quality champagne-method sparkling Brut and a broad all-round range of sound quality wines; owned by South Africa's richest mining conglomerate, Anglo-American Corporation. Their newly planted red-grape vineyards are promising; large, sprawling landholdings with a range of climates and soils. Production here already exceeds 300,000 cases a year.

Paarl

Fairview Estate – Often called the Cape's most adventurous winemaker, Charles Back bottles under an eclectic array of labels, but is best-known for exceptional Shiraz and a fine Pinotage. His range is notable for its generous, accessible drinkability at competitive prices. Close personal vineyard supervision by Back, who keeps in touch with world market trends.

Glen Carlou – Firm, dry, bold Chardonnays earned the Finlaysons an international reputation as well as a partnership investment from Napa's Donald Hess, of the Hess Collection, in 1996. Noted for production of distinctive Cabernet, Merlot and surprisingly successful and fruity Pinot Noir, considering this is a warm and dry growing zone.

Nederburg Wines – This is the Cape's biggest single independent (non cooperative) wine producer under one label. Nederburg sources grapes widely throughout Paarl and Stellenbosch. These unpretentious wines cover all ranges of style and quality, generally offering good value for money.

De Leeuwenjagt Wines – Promising producer of softer, modern red blend, Cabernet/Merlot and full, rich, supple Chardonnay with distinctive lemon-curd tones (in a 1996) and unusually fat, considerable Cape Riesling (Crouchen Blanc).

KWV (In Afrikaans, Wine Growers Co-operative Association) – Wines from the giant, controlling SA wine co-operative – unfussy, occasionally unexciting in the lower and middle orders, but more recently showing better balance, and some oak-imparted quality in top labels like Cathedral Cellar.

Veenwouden – Fashionable new vineyard and cellar owned by international tenor, Deon van der Walt; initially promising Cabernet/Merlot blends; should show even more style with Pomerol-based Frenchman Michel Rolland as consultant from 1996.

Plaisir de Merle – Probably nowhere in South Africa is supple Cabernet Sauvignon (with a dash of Merlot) ample and well-fleshed fruit more evident; riper, soft tannins a feature, from introductory 1993. Now a Merlot as well. Château Margaux's Paul Pontallier has been a consultant here since a complete makeover in the vineyards and cellar, post-1990.

Backsberg Estate – Established family farm, pioneering modern methods since early 1980s (especially in the vineyards, using American viticultural consultants) and leading producers of sound, well-priced Chardonnay, Cabernet, Pinotage, a good range of dessert wines especially Chenin Blanc; plus an unusual Malbec. This was the first estate producer of brandy to use Cognac formulae, a French-designed still and cask ageing.

Sonop Wines – Sells under Cape Levant labels; first-rate, plummy ripe Pinotage and dense, mint and berry-flavoured Cabernet. New Swiss-owned vineyards and winery have led to an emphasis on exports. Also a fuller range under Cape Soleil labels, including Chenin Blanc, Merlot and a good Pinotage.

Welgemeend Estate – Boutique-scale red-wine producer specialising in accessible, elegant Bordeaux-blend and a denser Malbec-based (with Cabernet, Merlot, Petit Verdot) blend; both red wines nicely barrel-aged.

Villiera Estate – Enterprising family operation recording solid successes on a broad front for the past decade. Notable wines include a champagne-method sparkling brut; a quality Sauvignon Blanc, from low-yielding, untrellised bush vines; also drinkable Merlot and a Cabernet/Merlot blend. The estate has built on some close contacts with French champagne growers. Competitive pricing.

Wellington

Claridge Wines – This boutique-sized, slightly eccentric winery has been rather unconventionally assembled by British immigrant Roger Jorgensen since 1991. He produces a dense, heavily-oaked Chardonnay and a red blend of Cabernet Sauvignon and Merlot named Wellington, which is grown in the foothills of Bains Pass. The red displays warm-climate no-nonsense tannic substance.

Swartland

Swartland Co-operative Winery – Versatile list from the hot wheatlands of the Cape, with unpretentiously big generous wines, produced in volume. The red Pinotage is a typical South African, thick-textured offering. The white wines, ranging from dry to sweet, are mainly Chenin Blanc-based; they represent good value and sometimes, when young, can be wonderfully fruity – if rather evanescent with age.

Tulbagh

Twee Jonge Gezellen Estate – Traditional Cape producer offering a big selection of off-dry and Muscat-based dessert white wines. Now also bottling some creditable champagne-method brut sparkling wine made from Chardonnay/Pinot Noir (50%/50%); and since 1995 involved in a partnership deal with Champagne Mumm. In occasional vintages, the estate also produces an outstanding botrytis dessert wine from a blend of white grapes.

Worcester

Nuy Co-operative Winery – This numbers among South Africa's smaller co-operatives, with just 25 member-growers, and it recently became the first to embark on an aggressive changeover from traditionally-planted varieties to the modern classics. Chardonnay, Sauvignon Blanc, Cabernet Sauvignon and Merlot, replacing the pedestrian and bulk varieties of the past. Until now they were bottling only non-vinifera table wine; for instance an off-dry white wine made from the extra-spicy Ferdinand de Lesseps grape, and labelled Chant de Nuy. They also regularly produce South Africa's finest examples of fortified red and white Muscadel;

and, in good years, there is a racy, guava-scented Colombard white wine.

Robertson

Graham Beck Winery (also Madeba labels) – From a futuristic cellar, no expenses-spared winery and extensive cooperage experiments, come some well-regarded Chardonnays and a bottle-fermented sparkling Blanc de Blancs (Chardonnay). Their naturally lime-rich soils are a help in a dry and warm arid region. The first (in 1996) evidence of lively, authentic Sauvignon Blanc from the Robertson region.

Zandvliet Estate – Known previously for hot climate, variable quality Shiraz, now (since 1995/96) turning out convincing, limey, lees-rich Chardonnay. Improving reds and blends.

Springfield Estate – Surprisingly good – for this hot, arid area – flavour-rich but neither fat nor flabby Cabernet Sauvignon; nicely oaked and with firm, medium-bodied structure. Also popular Sauvignon Blancs.

De Wetshof Estate – Five Chardonnays, varying from lightly oak-tinged to heavily toasted in flavour, made by the giant Danie de Wet, a sort of town crier and spokesman of the district on any and everything; he was the first in this region to introduce three varietals – Chardonnay, Sauvignon Blanc and Riesling – back in the late 1970s.

Bon Courage Estate – This roadside, Cape Dutch cellar makes a worthwhile stop; good value and a broad range. Wines vary from yeasty, lively Chardonnay/Pinot Noir based bottle-fermented dry sparkling wine (Jacques Bruére Brut) to two sumptuous dessert wines, a Gewürztraminer and even a fortified white Muscadel. Also produce some well-priced experiments such as blended Colombard/Chardonnay, and vin ordinaire in between.

Klein Karoo

Die Krans and Boplaas Estates – Two virtually contiguous estates, run by two branches of the Nel family (cousins) both specialising in vintage 'port' style wines, most lately incorporating Portugese Touriga Naçional with traditional Tinta Barocca; these are baking hot areas, with rich riverine soils, and dark, sweet, rich wines as a result. Close ties with the Symingtons family of Oporto.

△ *Fashionable Thelema Mountain Vineyards in Stellenbosch has Gyles Webb to thank for its quality status.*

North America

GRAPES HAVE ALWAYS GROWN IN NORTH AMERICA – the Vikings called it 'Vineland,' and if Columbus had reached the Florida mainland instead of the outer islands, he would have found a profusion of musky-tasting Scuppernongs.

Similar grapes provided early colonists with wine, which must have been pretty awful, because Lord Delaware imported grapevines and winemakers to Virginia from France in 1619. His efforts were the first of many failures, and eastern America and Canada had to muddle along with nasty native varieties and some hybrids created by crossing American and European varieties.

In California, the Spanish missionaries who arrived in 1769 brought seeds and cuttings of a European variety, mediocre but at least palatable. This was followed on a larger scale some 60 years later, in the 1830s, by Frenchmen who planted commercial vineyards using European grape varieties, and succeeded. The foundations of the US wine industry had been laid.

▽ California vineyards have survived the scourge of phylloxera and the impact of Prohibition to become a thriving industry.

The Gold Rush of 1849 brought hundreds of thousands of people to northern California from Europe in less than a decade, enough of whom had been involved in growing grapes and making wine to create an industry – by 1856, California wine was being shipped to England, Germany, Russia, Australia and China, and in 1869 the transcontinental railway opened up the eastern US market.

Almost parallel to this success was a scourge – Prohibition, a frenzied temperance movement that finally swept North America. Canada went dry in 1917, the US in 1920 creating a great social upheaval. Canada and many US states ended up with laws that severely restricted the making, marketing and advertising of wine, thus stunting the growth of the wine industry; the long break (ten years in Canada, 13 in the US) also meant a generation came of age misinformed about the history, traditions, and even the taste of wine. The effects lingered; it was only in the 1950s, after the Second World War, that modern winemaking really took off in the US.

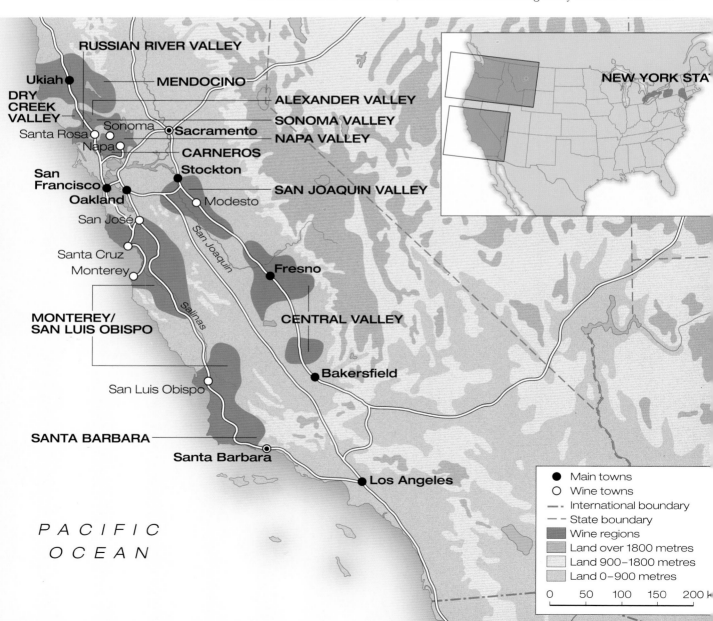

RUSSIAN RIVER VALLEY
Ukiah
DRY CREEK VALLEY
MENDOCINO
ALEXANDER VALLEY
SONOMA VALLEY
Santa Rosa   Sonoma
NAPA VALLEY
Napa   Sacramento
CARNEROS
San Francisco   Stockton
Oakland
SAN JOAQUIN VALLEY
San José   Modesto
Santa Cruz
Monterey
Fresno
MONTEREY/ SAN LUIS OBISPO
CENTRAL VALLEY
Salinas
San Luis Obispo
Bakersfield
SANTA BARBARA
Santa Barbara
Los Angeles

NEW YORK STATE

PACIFIC OCEAN

- ● Main towns
- ○ Wine towns
- –·– International boundary
- –– State boundary
- Wine regions
- Land over 1800 metres
- Land 900–1800 metres
- Land 0–900 metres

0   50   100   150   200 k

Today, wine is made in more than 40 of the 50 United States, including such unlikely-seeming places as Hawaii and Texas, and in several provinces of Canada, (see page 126). However, the leading wine-producing states are California, Washington, Oregon and New York (see page 124 for New York).

The wines of Washington and Oregon, often too casually lumped together as 'Northwest wines,' traced nearly the same arc as the wines of the eastern US; because European grapes had failed in the east, it was assumed for the most part in the mid-19th century that they wouldn't acclimatise in the west either.

Oregon's modern wine industry was started by a stubborn trio of mavericks: Richard Sommer, who was determined to make great Riesling, and came to Oregon for the cooler climate; David Lett, who was enamoured with Pinot Noir and Alsatian varieties; and Dick Erath, a home winemaker who bought grapes from Sommer, thought they were terrific and moved to Oregon to turn professional. That's pretty much the history in the 1960s and '70s, until new winemakers and a commitment to Pinot Noir created an industry. Washington made tentative moves at about the same time. A group of home winemakers and a winery with an uncertain future both decided to gamble on European grapes and the possibilities of fine wine when restrictive Prohibition-era laws were thrown out in 1969. It was an unlikely start to what has become a sophisticated industry.

California dominates the US wine scene, notching up seven out of every ten bottles sold in the US. As the wine business was always based on European varieties, little time was wasted getting to the heart of the matter – in fact, the problem more often was a surplus of grapes and wine, until phylloxera devastated crops in the 1880s, followed by Prohibition which threw things off the tracks again in the 1920s. The industry kept bouncing back, but often had to wait for the public to catch up. Only in 1968 did table wine finally outsell fortifieds, which led to a new wave of wineries rapidly advancing the fine wine ideal.

In 1978, a US government appellation system for US wine was instigated; it's rudimentary compared to some European regulations, but has generally led to improvements. Appellations are known officially as 'American Viticultural Areas,' or AVAs, and defined as 'delimited grape-growing regions distinguished by geographical features.' They are not definitions of quality. Wineries and grape-growers lay out their areas based on historical considerations, soil types, topography, political boundaries like town or county lines, and eventually most of the submissions are approved.

It operates basically as a series of increasingly restrictive circles. In the east and midwest of the US, where climate doesn't follow political subdivisions, multi-state appellations are allowed; there are also, everywhere, multi-county appellations, such as North Coast or Columbia Valley; counties, such as Sonoma or Santa Barbara, can be appellations; within them, valleys and mountains are also AVAs. At least 85 per cent of the grapes in these wines must come from the designated area. When a particular vineyard is named on the label, such as Bien Nacido Vineyard, 95 per cent of the grapes must come from there. As noted, it's not a guarantee of quality, but has elevated the approach to winemaking in the US in general. For a young industry, it's a good start.

△ Oregon's cool climate offers perfect conditions for growing the famously difficult Burgundian grape Pinot Noir.

California

California has a fascinating history of winemaking, going back through more than two centuries of struggle, of boom and bust, fortunes made and lost by a large cast of colourful characters, a landscape transformed forever, an entrepreneurial epic with just enough romance and idealism to keep it interesting. It's a grand story, but what is happening now is clearly a sequel; modern winemaking in California is a new and different game.

The state of California is larger than Italy, and has a wider range of soils and climates than any other winemaking nation in the world. Today, there are more than 800 wineries and contract winemakers producing wines from grapes that originated in France, Italy, Germany and Spain, as well as several crossbred varieties from a selection of these.

In the past, one could have described the California wine range as a rather wild and woolly patchwork, with a lot of hope and a little glory; today, California is divided between a fine-wine ideal that combines tradition and technology to achieve a standard of considerable excellence, and a market-driven commodity business that produces clean, sound, reliable wines representing good value for money. On occasion these may be middle-of-the-road and predictable, but they are often way ahead of their European counterparts.

Here, California is organised by specific areas that have established an identity and a standard, and in some cases even a style for their most notable wines. Some appellations, officially approved American Viticultural Areas, will be mentioned, but not all (not all, frankly, are entirely relevant yet, but express the politics of promise). One term to keep in mind is 'California' – wines bearing this appellation are usually blended from several areas, or may have been made in a winery in a different area from the winery that is selling it. They may be good value and are certainly always worth trying.

Carneros

Twenty years ago, Carneros was a nondescript patch on the way to the premier vineyard districts of Napa and Sonoma, an amorphous landscape of rolling hills and what appeared to be permanently tan-coloured grass. It would not have occurred to most observers that this sprawl might have boundaries and definition, let alone character, that could be expressed in something as elegant as wine.

Today, completely transformed, the Carneros district is one of California's best-known wine regions, its mission announced by the rows of vines regimented right down to the edges of its roads, providing texture and colour to the hills. This place is, at last, somewhere.

Geographically, it straddles Highway 12/121, an old stagecoach road between Sonoma and Napa, where the southern end of the Mayacamas mountain range slopes into the curve of San Pablo Bay, the topmost reach of the immense San Francisco Bay. Carneros is more cohesive than most wine areas. More than 80 per cent of the grapes grown in the area are either Chardonnay or Pinot Noir; the shallow soils are poor and rainfall sparse at the best of times, resulting in consistently low yields; the area is within the coolest classification defined by the University of California's heat-summation system; and the boundaries of the region are defined by topography, not politics. The sometimes elusive concept of terroir is alive and well here.

For many years, Carneros grapes and wines were used mostly to improve blends elsewhere, but in 1969 the tempo picked up – Buena Vista began planting a large vineyard within sight of San Pablo Bay, and the Sangiacomo family planted their now acclaimed vineyard. Winery Lake, planted in 1960 and one of the first vineyards to achieve label recognition, became better known than some of the wineries using its grapes. Carneros Creek Winery reintroduced the name of the former Spanish land grant from 1836, 'Rancho El Rincon de los Carneros,' the place where sheep roamed. As more vineyards were planted, the name Carneros became the reference point.

Another wave of wineries – Acacia, Bouchaine, Saintsbury and others – were formed in time for the beginnings of the appellation movement in the early 1980s.

△ *Vineyards belonging to Codorníu, the Californian arm of the famous Spanish cava producer, now making sparkling wine in Carneros.*

The Carneros appellation was approved in 1983 and was one of California's first. It is a multi-county appellation, part in Napa County, part in Sonoma. Soon afterwards, the wineries commissioned experiments at the University of California's oenology school, subjecting Pinot Noirs to descriptive analysis. Carneros wines were tasted against Napa and Sonoma wines, and statistical analysis showed that the Carneros examples clustered around certain flavours, while the others were scattered all over the chart. There was a clear Carneros style of Pinot Noir, noted the final report, 'generally high in fresh berry, berry jam, cherry and spicy aromas,' with a clear and 'unique' kinship among the wines' flavours.

All of this somewhat overshadowed the parallel success of Carneros Chardonnay, but the same focused flavour and cool-climate crispness manifested itself in a number of lean and racy wines, and was a major factor in drawing many wineries to the region during the land boom of 1987 to 1988: Clos du Val, Robert Mondavi, Shafer, Cuvaison and several others have settled in, and the expansion continues.

Sparkling wine also fitted in naturally in Carneros and swiftly gained an enthusiastic acceptance, while also knocking the rustic edges off the region with some international cachet. Domaine Chandon has extensive vineyards here, as does Domaine Mumm, while Domaine Carneros, Gloria Ferrer and Codorníu Napa have set up palatial wineries. The wines live up to the elegant premises.

Sonoma

Sonoma County is where wine-growing north of San Francisco really began. It also has a most colourful history, having been settled first by Russians who challenged Spain's claim, and then inherited by Mexico when Spain withdrew from empire-building. Sonoma had some Indian skirmishes, and declared itself a republic when the US went to war with Mexico in 1846. There were already thriving vineyards planted then.

Here most vineyards are situated close to the coast, and where the challenges of California's climate are the greatest. The elements to be considered are the cold fog that lingers out over the Pacific Ocean most of the year, the low mountains and hills jumbled together along the coast, and the San Francisco Bay, which helps draw the fog in when the heat of the interior valleys lowers the air pressure. The fog that freezes tourists in downtown San Francisco in August is actually optimal, beneficial air-conditioning for grapes. In Sonoma, late on a summer afternoon, you can see the fog roll in as swiftly and majestically unstoppable as an advancing avalanche.

Sonoma is large, with a variety of valleys and pockets. The Russian River, which flows through much of the county, adds another climatic complication. No other area has as many appellations and sub-appellations; as they often overlap or are tucked one into another the major ones are dealt with, from south to north.

Sonoma Valley

The Sonoma Valley is clearly defined, running between mountain ranges from the San Pablo Bay (it overlaps Carneros), up around the town of Sonoma, then in a northwesterly curve traced by Highway 12 nearly to Santa Rosa, a stretch of about

64 kilometres. Its proximity to San Francisco at the lower end and Santa Rosa at the top has made it a haven for commuters, so grapes vie for space with housing developments; in several areas, the developers have pre-empted prime vineyard land. (In the whole county, vineyard acreage has declined slightly of late.) It's also known as the Valley of the Moon, a name popularised by author Jack London, its most famous resident.

This is where the serious wine industry of northern California began, and several vineyards still thrive on those 150-year-old sites. There were some disruptions along the way, especially from phylloxera, which hit the area very hard in the 1870s when more than 400,000 dying vines had to be ripped out. The Sonoma Valley never regained the commanding position it had, although 100 years later it did regain considerable respect.

The southern part of the valley is fairly cool, often wrapped in pea-soup, bone-chilling fog until late on summer mornings. Zinfandel from this area is tough and tannic, certainly not for the faint-hearted, but Pinot Noir and Chardonnay do well. A little further north, around the town of Sonoma, the landscape becomes more rumpled, with the hills providing sun-catching slopes, and Zinfandel and Cabernet Sauvignon become more amenable. From here on, many of the vineyards are on hillsides, some merely bumps a few hundred metres high, some carved out of heavily forested mountains. There is a notable sub-AVA here, called rather plainly, 'Sonoma Mountain,' but better known for its vineyards: Jack London Ranch, McCrea, Laurel Glen's estate, and Benziger especially – and mostly known for fine Cabernet Sauvignon, with some superb Zinfandel and Chardonnay. In the northwest corner of the appellation, all alone and increasingly crowded by housing, is Matanzas Creek, known for Merlot, Chardonnay and Sauvignon Blanc.

Sebastiani is the largest winery in the Sonoma Valley, and by far; there are a few medium-sized operations (Kenwood and Chateau St Jean, for example), but most are relatively small, like Gundlach-Bundschu, Ravenswood, Arrowood, Carmenet and Kistler. It used to be decisively red-wine country, and still is on the whole, but now Chardonnay is the leading variety, as it is in so many other places.

Russian River Valley

Most of this appellation lies to the west of Highway 101 near Santa Rosa, with a small bulge further up to the east that is the Chalk Hill sub-AVA, best-known for full-bodied Chardonnay from the relatively warm hillsides. Much of this valley is actually a broad plain, an old seabed with a mix of soils, from alluvial dirt shifted during ancient floods, to gravel washed down rivers, to volcanic ash; this is where the Russian River veers sharply to the west, running at last into the Pacific Ocean, whose fogs surge back upstream and expand over the gently rolling hills, making this a very cool vineyard area – first-rate Pinot Noir and Chardonnay country.

It is also a fairly new wine-growing area, for much the same reason; the conditions are not easy here, for people or grapes. Cabernet Sauvignon and Zinfandel don't ripen well, if at all, in the lower half of the region (Sonoma-Green Valley sub-AVA). On the other hand, Pinot Noirs from here have a distinctive cherry-

△ *A bird's-eye view of Sonoma, which has more appellations and sub-appellations than any other California wine area.*

and-spice aspect and the Chardonnays are intense and racy. Given the climate, it was to be expected that many of those grapes would also go into excellent sparkling wine, some of California's best. Iron Horse has made a name for itself with good sparkling and table wines, and Marimar Torres made an immediate splash with a muscular Chardonnay and a lean Pinot Noir. DeLoach and Olivet Lane are two other well-known wineries here, while Sonoma-Cutrer, just to the north, is a Chardonnay specialist of renown.

Other wineries that have made a name for Russian River Pinot Noir include Rochioli and the now legendary Willams-Selyem, a tiny operation formerly housed in a garage operated by two easygoing guys and their families who happened to make some of the best Pinots in the US, using old-fashioned methods and working in small batches. Up in the northern half of the area, where the Russian River flows on a north-south axis, vineyards cluster on its banks and somehow full-blooded, intense and luscious Zinfandels emerge from in among the Pinot Noir and even some Gewürztraminer, another cool-loving grape that does especially well here. There are also small patches yielding good Sauvignon Blanc. One anomaly, and a nice one, is the dark, firm Petite Sirah from Foppiano. In Europe, few of these grapes grow well together, and no one is sure why they do here; but no one bemoans the fact.

Dry Creek Valley

The Dry Creek Valley begins at a point just south of Healdsburg, where the stream of Dry Creek runs into the Russian River at an opposing angle to westward. The landscape is wilder here; the valley is narrow, with steep hillsides rising up to the west, thick forests and quick-draining volcanic soils. The climate is cool. This area was settled more than 100 years ago mostly by Italian immigrants who established small farms, growing apples, prunes, various vegetables and grapes. Today, you'll find wall-to-wall vineyards between Dry Creek Road and West Dry Creek Road, which run parallel the length of the valley. There are no towns, no developments, little traffic; it's pleasantly quiet in other words.

This is, first and foremost, Zinfandel country. There is also a lot of Cabernet Sauvignon, often very good and something of a threat in light of its popularity, but Zinfandel is still holding on. It tends to be a big wine here, voluptuously fruity but firm, and with an underlying elegance – benchmark Zinfandel in other words. This is where Nalle's splendid small supply of wines comes from, and where Lytton Springs is found, one of the oldest vineyards in Sonoma and now owned by Ridge Vineyards. Quivira and Rafanelli are across the valley, also upholding the standard. Much further to the north is Pedroncelli, one of the area's oldest wineries, producing more restrained but still tasty Zinfandel. Dry Creek Vineyards, which began the modern winery era in 1972, produces a range of superb wines, which of course includes Zinfandel.

This is also where E&J Gallo has set up headquarters for its Sonoma holdings – it is the largest owner of grapevine acreage in the county. The vineyards are large and well-groomed, and several are organically farmed. The winery is spinning off a range of different brands from varying appellations now, and apparently evolving its approach to fine wine, so generalisations about specific wines are difficult. Nevertheless, I once tasted a freshly bottled, unblended Zinfandel from Gallo's Dry Creek vineyard, and it was extraordinary, one of the best I've ever tasted. When it finally came to market a year later, it was not nearly as good, perhaps from blending or some other tinkering, but I'll never forget that initial, direct, lovely wine. Someday, perhaps, it will emerge again.

Cabernet Sauvignon from Dry Creek Valley is slightly herbaceous and generally good for ageing. Besides some of the above wineries, Ferrari-Carano and William Wheeler have also added to that roster with distinction. Preston Vineyard and Duxoup, up in the northern corner, go their own, individual way with Rhône-style and rustic-Italian-style wines. In the hills above, the Bradford Mountain vineyard supplies excellent Merlot and Cabernet Franc to several wineries, notably Ridge and Chateau Souverain.

Alexander Valley

Just to the northeastern side of the Dry Creek Valley above Healdsburg, and sharing a boundary with that district along the ridge line, the Alexander Valley runs parallel to Highway 101 for some 20 kilometres, following the course of the Russian River. The Pacific Ocean fogs that chill the regions downstream don't reach this far up, and the valley is wide, sun-washed and significantly warmer. The soils here are a mix of gravel, loam, sand, clay and good-sized rocks, whatever washes down when the river floods and overflows its banks, which is every few years.

It was settled in the 1840s, as naturally good farming land, and in 1880 became the site of a curious social experiment that influenced its character greatly. A San Francisco banker of Italian origin set up the Italian Swiss Colony as a cooperative vineyard for unemployed Italian and Swiss labourers. They were given room, board and wages, from which US$5 a month would be deducted as a credit toward stock in the company. In 25 years, they were promised a substantial stake and ownership of some land. After a short while, the 'colonists' rebelled, deciding

△ *Above left: The barrique cellar of Ferrari-Carano, Dry Creek Valley. Zinfandel (above) is the dominant grape variety in this area.*

it was all a scam and demanding full pay instead of stock. The vineyard and winery became a corporation, eventually the third biggest winery in the US, and its investors became very rich. In the meantime, many of the workers and their children settled throughout the county, giving it a rural, Italianate, agricultural character that persists to an extent.

Cabernet Sauvignon has made the reputation of the Alexander Valley, and it is notably rich and supple, leaning a little toward herbaceousness when young: Alexander Valley Vineyards, Simi, Jordan, Clos du Bois, Estancia, Murphy-Goode, Geyser Peak and Napa's Silver Oak are good examples. Much Merlot was planted for Bordeaux-type blends by some of the more ambitious newcomers, and has also performed well enough to be bottled on its own. Here and there, Zinfandel shines through brightly, especially on the Geyserville patch well utilised by Ridge, and by Sausal, a small winery whose Zinfandels are some of California's best and are well worth seeking out.

Chardonnay is successfully grown in the southern end, coming up rich and generous, tending toward butterscotch at times, but in cool years simply ample and apple-crisp. There have also been enough creamy Sauvignon Blancs from the poor and gravelly soils near the river to command attention. The top end of the valley is the northernmost point in the US where oranges will grow; the landscape is made up of smoothly rolling hills and is the only place in Sonoma County that looks prim and proper. It is in fact another, huge, Gallo vineyard. The company bought earthmoving equipment, scraped off a layer of top soil, rearranged the hills to their satisfaction, put the top soil back, and planted neat vineyards; but as yet there have been no Alexander Valley bottlings.

Napa Valley

Driving through the Napa Valley, admiring the neatly manicured rows of grapevines that make an orderly pattern on the valley floor and up into the foothills on either side, it's easy to accept the assessment of an early historian, who called this place 'a paradise for the vine'. Many of the winery buildings are architectural showcases, from Robert Mondavi's Mission-style compound, to Sterling's mock Greek monastery, to Opus One's Martian-spaceship-meets-Greek-temple. Restaurants are stylish, booked solid, expensive; tasting rooms are full of keen consumers, eagerly consuming. Commodity grape-growers and bulk winemakers from outside the valley look at all this and call it 'the Disneyland of the wine business'. Locals just smile; they're at the top of the pyramid, in the premier wine area of the US, the place most people mean when they say they've visited 'wine country.'

Getting to this stage was not easy – Napa has had higher surges and lower fall-offs than many other areas that have survived as wine-growing districts. For one thing, it started late; initially no one seemed to think Napa had much promise except as grazing land for cattle, and perhaps wheat fields. The first settlers established vineyards mainly for their own use, but the wine boom in Sonoma after the gold rush in 1849 set off an explosion of commerce here; in little more than a decade there were 50 wineries in Napa Valley, which also became a popular resort for tourists, despite the fact that getting there took two days by train, ferryboat and stagecoach from major cities. (Robert Louis Stevenson honeymooned there and wrote the first draft of *Treasure Island*, as well as an essay that spread Napa's fame to Europe.)

Then phylloxera struck. The root louse, which devastates grapevines, hit Napa's vineyards especially hard because they had the largest percentage of susceptible European varieties growing close together. Wine grape acreage dropped from more than 81,000 hectares to less than 202 hectares in a decade. Ironically, the reputation of Napa Valley wines, especially reds, was booming, even while pioneering vintners were going broke. The comeback after the turn of the century, when phylloxera seemed to be beaten, was spectacular, but just around the corner lurked the bigger threat of Prohibition. That second blow was really hard – some people started growing prunes or pears, others tore out fine-wine grapes and planted table grapes. It was not until the early 1970s, when the whole state experienced a boom, that wine grape plantings returned to the level of nearly 100 years before.

△ *Stag's Leap District: in 1976 wines from here came top in a Parisian tasting, putting California on the world wine map.*

Today, there are about 220 wineries farming more than 13,000 hectares of vines, and there is little room for expansion. The 1980s saw a hideous flashback when a new strain of phylloxera, a 'super-louse', appeared. Affected vines were torn out and burned, new types of rootstock replanted, and many wineries took the opportunity to also replant new varieties in new patterns, often using the European model of putting in more vines per acre – they get a little more quantity, and a lot more quality. The expense has been horrendous (and we consumers will all get to share that), but the benefits should be considerable.

In the early days, Napa was especially noted for red wines in the 'claret' style, at first made from Zinfandel, but later from Cabernet Sauvignon. Today, it approaches a Bordeaux ideal more strongly than ever: more than 4,000 hectares are planted to Cabernet Sauvignon, 1,800 hectares to Merlot, 300 hectares to Cabernet Franc and small amounts to Malbec and Petit Verdot, amounting to nearly half of all the valley's grapes (and a considerable increase in those Bordeaux varieties over the last ten years). The expansion has come largely at the expense of white wine grape varieties, all of which are down in acreage except Chardonnay and small patches of the newly fashionable Pinot Gris and Viognier.

The Napa Valley is some 40 kilometres long and eight kilometres wide at best, ranging in a northwesterly arc that gently curves up and away from the San Francisco Bay. It follows the bed of the Napa River, which doesn't seem like much of a stream until it rains for several weeks in February and can then flood the valley floor, as it does three or four times in a decade. The southern end of the Napa Valley is cooler than the northern, because of the fog from the bay, and is coolest in the Carneros district (see page 101), which is officially part of the Napa Valley AVA.

There are a number of sub-AVAs within what became a rather wide definition of 'Napa Valley' when the appellation was being drawn, in a heated debates. There would be more if all winemakers had had their way, as such decisions can have considerable economic impact on a winery's fortunes – boundaries of desirable appellations, such as Stag's Leap District and Rutherford-Oakville, have become quite elasticised over years of argument. Obviously, some are more valid than others in terms of grape-growing, while others are so new (or newly replanted) that it is too soon to tell. In many instances, the names of individual vineyards have achieved a status close to that of AVAs, pre-empting the issue. The level of winemaking here is high, certainly, but the best assurance, as everywhere, is the name of the winery.

After Carneros, vineyards proliferate above the town of Napa. In the mountains to the west, in the Mount Veeder sub-AVA, Cabernet and Chardonnay grow well, as shown by the original pioneer, Mayacamas, and a newcomer, The Hess Collection (named after the art gallery in the winery, not a bunch of grapes). On the valley floor, on a long unbroken reach, vineyards are mostly planted with excellent Chardonnay that finds its way to quite a few wineries.

Along the Silverado Trail, the quiet road that runs up the east side of the valley, is the Stag's Leap District. Here, Warren Winiarski established Stag's Leap Wine Cellars, which came top in the 1976 wine tasting in Paris and established California wines as world-class. Another winery was founded also called Stags' Leap (notice the

wandering apostrophe), which led to lawsuits. When other wineries began using 'Stag's Leap' as an unofficial appellation, there were more lawsuits and a formal appellation was proposed. However, once the boundaries were drawn, nearby vineyards who were left out threatened lawsuits. The whole business took more than ten years to resolve. Today this area is devoted mostly to Cabernet that is outstanding in quality, especially from Stag's Leap Wine Cellars, Clos du Val, Pine Ridge, Silverado Vineyards, and Shafer, which also turns out some of the best Merlots in California.

The centre of the Napa Valley is the gold coast, millionaires' row, top of the pops, a gallery of world-famous names, both wineries and vineyards. Some of California's most expensive Cabernets have come from Martha's Vineyard, Napanook, BV 1 and 2, Bosche and Bella Oaks. The two built-up intersections known officially as towns are Oakville and Rutherford, both considered definite sub-AVAs despite arguments over where one stopped and the other began. A good deal of the history of the valley, old and new, is found here along Highway 29, from Inglenook (now owned by movie director Francis Ford Coppola) and Beaulieu, to Robert Mondavi, Far Niente, Cakebread, Grgich Hills, Franciscan, Caymus, Louis Martini and others not quite as well-known. Along the Silverado Trail across the valley are ZD, Heitz and Phelps. All make a variety of wines, and quite well too, but outstanding in all cases are the powerful, emphatic Cabernets. High above, on Howell Mountain, superb Cabernet and Merlot justify its AVA status.

Above the town of St Helena, the hills crowd the highway on the west as the valley narrows, and vineyards are mostly situated on the east side of the road. The exception is the Spring Mountain AVA, which is set way up in the hills and harbours several small wineries. Beringer's elaborate, 100-year-old-plus Rhine House can be found here, as can Freemark Abbey, Duckhorn, Sterling, Diamond Creek, Cuvaison and Chateau Montelena. Sparkling wine specialist Schramsberg is tucked up in the western hills near here, high and cool enough for Pinot Noir to grow well and perfect for combining with Chardonnay, from down the valley, to make classic wines.

As good as Chardonnay and Cabernet Sauvignon are in the Napa Valley, they're far from the whole story. There is much fine Zinfandel, with Frog's Leap, Caymus, Burgess and Clos du Val proving this consistently. Sangiovese has also made a terrific start, notably from Atlas Peak, a one-winery sub-AVA in the eastern hills, and from Robert Pepi, Rodeno, Swanson and Franciscan. Sauvignon Blanc, also known as Fumé Blanc, can be wonderful here, fresh and crisp and only lightly grassy or herbal, often leaning more to flavours of melon and aromas that are lightly floral – Frog's Leap and Grgich Hills are good examples. Robert Mondavi's well-known Fumé Blanc is more structured, fuller, partly from oak, partly from a little Sémillon blended in. Indeed, the problem has never been the quality of the Sauvignon Blanc here; the problem is, inevitably, the popularity of Chardonnay.

In 1880, Robert Louis Stevenson wrote, 'One corner of land after another is tried with one kind of grape after another. This is a failure; that is better; a third best. So, bit by bit, they grope about for their Clos Vougeot and Lafite ... The smack of Californian earth shall linger on the palate of your grandson.' In the Napa Valley, a lot of people feel that the search is over.

CALIFORNIA

△ Inglenook Winery, on Highway 29 is co-owned by film director Francis Ford Coppola.

Mendocino

Mendocino is part of the earliest history of California settlement, dating back to the first European discovery, by Spanish sea captain Juan Cabrillo in 1542. Both the coast and the interior must have seemed somewhat forbidding – fog and rocks complicated landings and the rugged forests of towering fir and redwood trees seemed impenetrable – so it was not settled until the early 19th century, when Mexico and Russia nearly went to war over it.

Mendocino has always been a place for the bold. In the absence of roads, early lumber barons sent their sawn wood to San Francisco and Los Angeles by ship; fishermen ranged from there to Alaska, by sail; when roads were built, Black Bart, the legendary highwayman, used to commute the 160 kilometres from San Francisco to rob stagecoaches. Today, the leading cash crop is reputed to be marijuana, grown back in the still sparsely populated hills.

Wine came fairly late to Mendocino, after the loggers cleared much of the forest, as one of several crops, in about the 1880s. Little is known about the wine then, as it was mostly sold in bulk, although some records indicate that wineries in the Napa Valley paid a premium for Mendocino red grapes, to improve what they called their 'claret'. The relative anonymity meant that when Prohibition wiped out the wine industry there, it more or less disappeared for good. Only Parducci, founded in the 1930s, kept the faith until the wine boom of the 1960s, when it was joined by Fetzer.

There are several vineyard areas in Mendocino, quite distinct even if not always distinctive (which may also be attributable to travelling grapes and blending from various areas). The inland area follows the Russian River – and, inevitably, Highway 101 most of the way – and the coastal area, known as the Anderson Valley, veers off sharply to the ocean and the pretty town of Mendocino along Highway 128.

The inland area, above and below the large town of Ukiah, has a somewhat quirky climate – it's wet in the winter and hot in summer – but the growing season is shortened by the rainstorms and cold fronts at either end. Cabernet Sauvignon and Zinfandel usually have a bright fruitiness and berry freshness, although a few

individual vineyards in the hills have been known to stretch to power and ageability. Chardonnay and Sauvignon Blanc can be outstanding. The McDowell Valley AVA is quite small and home to a winery of the same name which found notoriety producing luscious Rhône-style wines, including first-rate Syrah from old vines, and appears to be flourishing under new owners. Further north, Chardonnay and Pinot Noir barely ripen, making them ideal for sparkling wines, most notably Scharffenberger's.

The two powers in the area, Parducci and Fetzer, have recently undergone some changes. The Parducci family sold shares in the winery, and became embroiled in conflicts with its partners; the future seems uncertain, but the vineyards are excellent and the winemaking facilities have been upgraded, so the potential for continuing to produce reliable wines remains. Fetzer was one of the world's great wine business success stories, going from a simple small family vineyard to a multi-million-litre winery in 20 years. It popularised Gewürztraminer (which everyone thought was impossible) until it was selling more than 150,000 cases a year. Fetzer also marketed wines that blended Washington and Oregon grapes with Californian grapes, most notably, the company made a major commitment to organic farming. In 1992, Fetzer sold the winery, for a reported US$100 million, to a large wine and spirits corporation but kept a reasonable amount of vineyard. It now sell grapes back to the winery, which seems to be continuing the commitment to quality. Among a bewildering variety of wines, those designated 'Barrel Select' and 'Reserve' usually show real excellence.

The other notable area, Anderson Valley, is an extremely pretty, narrow groove through majestically forested mountains, some 40 kilometres long and three miles wide. Here America's best Gewürztraminer can be found, made by several wineries, benefiting from the fogs that regularly roll down the valley. The reputation of the area is being created by sparkling wine, however, as Roederer and Scharffenberger produce consistently fine wines from Pinot Noir and Chardonnay. Most of the other wineries are small, and some have changed owners lately, so future directions are difficult to assess.

△ *Once long-isolated, the narrow Anderson Valley is renowned today for its Gewürztraminer and sparkling wines.*

Central Coast

The Central Coast AVA is enormous, covering the territory from just south of San Francisco to Santa Barbara, amounting to seven fairly large counties. There is enough similarity in growing conditions to begin to justify the appellation, although some not entirely relevant history and politics also came into play when it was created. As a catch-all, Central Coast has sufficient logic to it, and there are several smaller AVAs within this huge area that are clearly defined in terms of character.

East of San Francisco, over the hills and clear of the fog, is the Livermore Valley where the Wente family have been making wine for more than 100 years, mostly white, with clear, correct varietal character. Property developers who want to uproot vineyards to build commuter housing are the biggest hazard in Livermore, and the Wentes have bought two other wineries to preserve the open space. Lately, Randall Grahm has also moved in, taking over a failed winery and vineyard.

The majority of the grapes in the Central Coast are grown in Monterey County, in large vineyards. This is the countryside John Steinbeck made famous in *East of Eden* and other books, a long, wide valley with rich soil. It had no history of grape-growing because rainfall is low, and strong winds, thought to be a danger to vines, blow through the length of the valley nearly every afternoon. In the early 1960s, vintners from Santa Clara (which was fast becoming the highly developed Silicon Valley) and Livermore Valley discovered solutions to the climatic problems: The Salinas River, flowing beneath the ground, provided plenty of water for overhead sprinkling and drip-irrigation systems, and vines were planted parallel to the path of the wind. Monterey went from just 2.5 hectares or so to 14,000 hectares by 1983.

Much of the area was owned by corporations for whom ensuring a return on investment meant planting what sold best. So Cabernet Sauvignon was king, followed closely by Chardonnay. The trouble was, the Cabernet ended up tasting like celery-and-cabbage tonic and it took a while to find a solution to make them palatable, which had to do with the timing and amount of irrigation. Today, Monterey plantings have dropped to 11,700 hectares, and the majority of the grapes grown are

white. Nearly half are Chardonnay, which makes perfectly serviceable wine; but the real strengths here are Riesling, Gewürztraminer and Pinot Blanc.

There are not many wineries in this stretch, which has compounded the identity problem. One solution, for some, was to create smaller AVAs, most of which don't have enough of a track record yet. Some show promise though, including the Carmel Valley, tucked behind steep hills that give it some distinctiveness, and Paso Robles, situated sufficiently inland to be warmer.

Two appellations deserve particular attention. The wineries that created them are situated high above the valley floor, working under difficult conditions, and the wines they produce are basically Burgundian. Chalone is both a winery and an AVA, its vineyards some 503 metres up in the mountains; high enough to look down on the fog banks and cooled by the breezes, but sun-soaked. The chunky volcanic soils found here are shot through with limestone and are quite poor. What's more, it is so dry that water has to be trucked in ... and the operation did not have a telephone until recently. Going there is like visiting a monastery of a particularly ascetic sect. The wines produced are Pinot Noir and Chardonnay, intense and brooding.

Mt Harlan is also a one-winery appellation, the home of Calera, which is devoted to Pinot Noir. It is situated some 610 metres up, just along the same mountain range as Chalone, though in a different county, San Benito. Owner Josh Jensen makes several single-vineyard wines either from this appellation or the San Benito AVA. He has also been turning out some distinctive Viognier. Both Chalone and Calera are much sought after, and may account for the fact that others in the Monterey and San Benito foothills are turning to Pinot Noir; early examples have shown great promise.

Santa Barbara

Like Monterey, Santa Barbara was one of the most important and civilised cities in California in the 18th and 19th centuries, when Los Angeles was a rowdy Wild West town and San Francisco a sparsely populated, fogbound sandspit. Santa Barbara county was, and is, a setting of great beauty, with tree-lined hillsides above miles of

△ *Firestone Vineyards in Santa Ynez Valley, Santa Barbara, which has recently invested in new Pinot Noir plantings.*

sandy beaches; the city of Santa Barbara has preserved three of the original Spanish Missions, and much of the architecture duplicates the beautiful simplicity of the style. It is a gracious place – the contrast with smoggy, overbuilt Los Angeles, only 145 kilometres south, is striking.

Santa Barbara is unique along the entire coast of North America for having the only east-west traverse of coastline, as it suddenly veers off at a sharp right angle for 80 kilometres, so that it is bound on two sides by the ocean. From the air, the landscape looks crudely carved, as it was – by prehistoric glaciers, volcanic upheavals and surging rivers. A series of gaps and passes steadily draw in the ocean fog and cool breezes, to the point where this part of southern California is actually as cool, on average, as Burgundy.

For much of its history, wine made here was sold off in bulk, and Prohibition ended what little industry there was. In the 1960s, vines were planted again, and the first wines were so good that they set off a boom. Unfortunately, the taste of the US public was just being formed, and Santa Barbara went in what became the wrong direction. The Riesling and Gewürztraminer were superb, but not enough people cared for them. Cabernet Sauvignon and Sauvignon Blanc, which the public did want, tasted herbal at best. Fortunately, Chardonnay also grew quite well, as did Pinot Noir and in the last ten years, the trend to these two grapes has accelerated – Chardonnay plantings have more than doubled, at the expense of all other whites, and Pinot Noir vineyards have also increased.

Santa Maria

Santa Maria has two very different AVAs. The Santa Maria Valley is home to large vineyards that were essentially corporate farming ventures, selling grapes to wineries outside the area, mostly Chardonnay and well regarded for their clear, direct, lightly citric flavour. In the late 1980s, Robert Mondavi, Kendall-Jackson and Beringer bought these large parcels and Mondavi also bought Byron Vineyard & Winery, a respected producer of Pinot Noir, and left the winemaker in charge. Just to the north of these large holdings is the independent vineyard called Bien Nacido (meaning, roughly, 'good and natural', which must be accurate, as a dozen wineries buy their grapes and put the name on their labels). Next door are two small fine wineries: Au Bon Climat, devoted to Pinot Noir and Chardonnay, and Qupé, well-respected for Syrah and now moving into superb Rhône-style white wines as well.

The other AVA, Santa Ynez Valley, is more complicated, with smaller wineries, most of which have not made as much of a name for themselves as they deserve. There is much excellent Pinot Noir and Chardonnay grown here, and an increasing emphasis on Rhône varieties; the best-known wineries are Firestone and Sanford.

San Joaquin Valley

As big as the San Joaquin Valley is – more than 320 kilometres long and an average width of nearly 80 kilometres – it's only about half the size of California's Central Valley. Today, San Joaquin Valley is an agricultural wonder, growing more than 200 different types of crops of fruit, nuts and vegetables on enormous farms.

The history of the hot and dry San Joaquin Valley is fairly brief. Most of the colonisation was along the more hospitable coast until the 1850s, when the gold rush brought hundreds of thousands of people to California. Some settled along the valley's rivers and established large farms. Wheat was the main crop until irrigation systems were developed in the 1870s, when grapes led the rush to diversity. It was always a commodity business – the Thompson Seedless grape was popular, as it could be eaten as a table grape, dried into raisins, fermented into quite bland but palatable wine, and distilled into brandy. The most popular real wine grape was 'West's White Prolific', also known as French Colombard – a grape distilled into Cognac in France, but having the virtue of retaining acidity in a hot climate, producing a neutral wine with a fresh, perfumed aroma.

This is also where California's dessert wines came from, as quite a few Spanish settled here, planting Palomino, Pedro Ximenes, Valdepeñas, several Muscats and other similar grapes. As the market for fortified sweet wines has declined, most vineyards have been grafted over to table-wine varieties, but a few diehards soldier on, notably Andrew Quady, who makes delicious Black and Orange Muscat, and a port-type wine he calls 'Starboard'.

The wine business here is unromantic. Its commodity nature is signalled by clusters of towering stainless steel tanks lining the arrow-straight roads that cross the monotonous plains. Wineries here are multi-million-litre enterprises, spic and span, computerised, with huge pumps moving wine through endless pipelines. The vineyards are immense, thousands of acres of vines with black irrigation pipes snaking down each long, precise row. At night, monstrous shapes crawl the vineyards, bright eyes gleaming as they roar – mechanical harvesters, shaking the grapes off the vines, onto conveyor belts that carry them to open gondolas behind.

There's not too much point in talking about territory here. This is where plonk, known as 'jug wine', comes from. The most popular grape is still French Colombard, increasingly known simply as Colombard, followed by Chenin Blanc which in this heat is fairly neutral but slightly fruity. Zinfandel can take the heat and is on the increase, undoubtedly because of the boom in lightly sweet 'White' Zinfandel. The San Joaquin contains a little more than half the total of California's wine grape acreage, but produces much more than half the wine because of the higher yields per acre than in the fine-wine districts – well over two million tonnes are crushed every year. It is cheap and usually cheerful, clean and sound at least. These are wines that bear the 'California' appellation, often bottled under contract to well-known wineries.

Two districts are worth some attention, both at the top of the valley, cooled by breezes off the Sacramento River delta. Lodi is one, an AVA that was long famous for rich Zinfandels, but is now better known, thanks to Robert Mondavi, as Woodbridge. This is where his low-priced everyday wines are made. Sebastiani also has a similar operation down the road. The second, the Clarksburg AVA, is to the west and comprises an odd collection of vineyards that sit behind levees below the water level on islands in the Sacramento River; it once produced quality Chenin Blanc, quite lovely wine, but has now been overrun by mediocre Chardonnay, which sells for a higher price. Madness. Someday, maybe it will revert to its proper destiny.

△ *Above left: Au Bon Climat, Santa Barbara, where Jim Clendenen makes fine Chardonnay and Pinot Noir.*

Washington

Washington State was a legendary wilderness for a long time, as elusive as a myth to seafaring explorers. Sir Francis Drake missed it in 1579, repelled by 'the most vile, thicke and stinking fogges,' and Captain James Cook had no better luck 200 years later. (Despite that, England attempted to lay claim to whatever was lurking back there anyway.) The actual settlers, the 'gentlemen adventurers' of the Hudson's Bay Company, slipped in by land, drifting down from Canada and making fortunes from fishing, logging and furs. It was hard, raw, rough country, well suited to brash entrepreneurs; agriculture was merely an afterthought.

Washington has always been just a little different and has gone its own way. It does rain a lot in the winter on the west side of the state where most of the people live, and can seem gloomy (it has been called the 'spectacularly mildewed corner of the American carpet'). 'Twin Peaks', US television's most offbeat drama, was set here. In 1948, an Air Force pilot flying past Mount Rainier saw what became known as Unidentified Flying Objects. Ramtha, a 30,000-year-old spirit in the body of a housewife with a fondness for Atlantis myths and a flair for evangelical marketing of her prophecies, lives nearby. These may all be related occurrences.

This is also where the original Skid Row was (the term was originally Skid Road, a slipway for logs from the hills down to the waterfront in Seattle, where they were loaded on barges; it was also an unsavoury part of town). Grapes were grown here from the mid-19th century onwards, but they were native American varieties, good only for grape juice and jelly, although that did not stop some people from making them into fairly unpleasant wine. When Prohibition ended, a monopoly system for selling wine was set up – you could only buy from a state store, and extra taxes were imposed on out-of-state and foreign wines, to protect the locals. It took years of lawsuits before Washington became a free market, in 1969. That is effectively when the modern wine industry began.

Some farmers had planted vineyards with proper grapes, but the only market for them was wineries making dessert wines, fairly foul concoctions that blended European vinifera varieties with the native types, fortified with grain alcohol. When the law was changed, a group of home winemakers took a chance and turned professional, making decent wines from the proper grapes; they were professors from the University of Washington, and their small venture eventually became the Columbia Winery. At the same time, a commercial winery brought in the great Californian winemaker Andre Tchelistcheff and gave him a free hand to create some good wines – that operation became Chateau Ste Michelle. None of us who remember those early days could ever have guessed that the Washington wine industry would come as far as it has – all the way to a world-class standard, and a good size – from that bizarre and hesitant beginning. It is a case of the 'gentlemen adventurers' all over again, and perhaps, in retrospect, it was inevitable.

Like Oregon, Washington is wet to the west and dry to the east of the Cascade Mountains. There are a few small vineyards on the west side, but several wineries which, large and small, get most of their grapes from the dry east side. The small ones tend to hand-craft wines, mostly from Cabernet Sauvignon and Merlot, but there have also been notable Rieslings and one Nebbiolo. The large wineries are mostly showplaces and tasting rooms now, with gardens and picnic facilities, intended to present a public presence to the largest possible population, with some space given over to ageing cellars, while the wine is actually made in no-frills facilities out on the east side.

Driving across the eastern desert is an experience not to be forgotten, and one I wouldn't want to do too often. After a monotony of vast wheat fields, there are endless kilometres of sagebrush; a lonesome cowboy on horseback would not be out of place. Then, suddenly, there are neat squares and rectangles of green: fields of hops, mint, asparagus, berries, orchards of cherry, apple and peach trees and the familiar rows of grapevines. The average rainfall is a bit less than 205 millimetres a year, but the Columbia River, America's second largest at 2,000 kilometres long and

△ *Above left: Sunset over Columbia River. Above: Arctic freezes can devastate crops in Washington, so grape varieties must be chosen with care.*

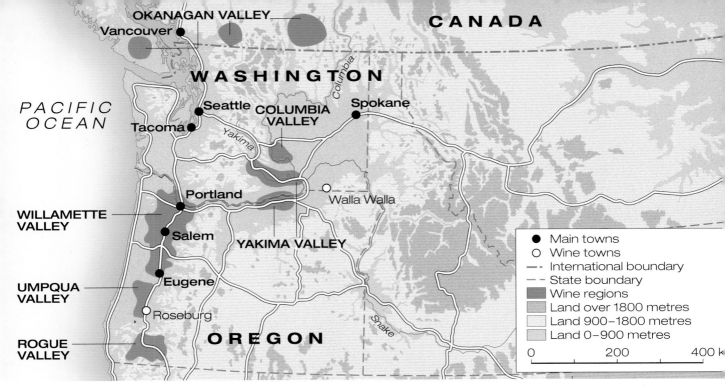

forming the border between Oregon and Washington, provides a lifeline of irrigation. The climate here swings through extremes – roasting on a long midsummer day, a 20°C drop by midnight. The fruit can handle such dramatic changes better than we do, with the apples, cherries and grapes popping with lively acidity that bolsters the considerable, direct flavours.

There are only a few appellations in Washington so far, but they are quite large: Yakima Valley comprises 260,000 hectares, though only a bit more than 2,000 are under vine at the moment, and Walla Walla has 72,470 hectares, with just 36 hectares in half a dozen vineyards. Surrounding both these areas is the Columbia Valley AVA, which accounts for nearly 4.5 million hectares (about 28,962 square kilometres), of which only 7,280 are planted vineyards (not counting the totals from the other two areas). The amount of land suitable for cultivation is thought to be considerable, so there's plenty of room to grow. There are wineries near Spokane, at the eastern edge of the state, but the wine is made mostly from grapes purchased elsewhere; Puget Sound, around Seattle, has just received an AVA, but its effect remains to be seen.

Regional differences within Washington are not so vast so far. Grape-growing here is quite market-driven, but there's another consideration: At least once a decade, sometimes twice, there come killing Arctic freezes, so severe that you can hear trees crack in the middle of the night; in the early days of small-scale vineyards, it was common practice to pile dirt and straw over the vines in November and dig them out in March, for rudimentary protection. Growers today survive by planting other crops, by charting the air flow for beneficial currents, and by treading a fine line between planting varieties the market wants and those that will survive best. (The sad thing, for example, is that Riesling is a hardy variety and makes excellent wine here, but consumers don't care for it – so there's a surplus.)

Another factor that keeps generalisations from sitting still is the rapid expansion of vineyards, and changes in the fortunes of some varieties. Riesling acreage has decreased somewhat over the last decade, as has Chenin Blanc and Gewürztraminer; all often made good wines, but none are much loved by

decreased somewhat over the last decade, as have those of Chenin Blanc and Gewürztraminer; all often made good wines, but none are much loved by consumers. In contrast the amount of vineyard planted out to Chardonnay has more than doubled. A trend is a trend, and Washington Chardonnay is good enough, even sometimes very good. The best white wine here, though, may be Sémillon, which seems to be partly holding its own due to an increase in Australian-style blends with Chardonnay (but resulting in better, fuller and firmer).

The overall star, increasingly, is abundantly fruity and increasingly fine Merlot, which is now the leading red grape variety (Chardonnay and Merlot account for nearly half of all the vineyard area). Cabernet Sauvignon has been successful at times, and is not losing ground, and Cabernet Franc is now up and coming, so a Bordeaux future seems likely. The light and fruity red that every wine area needs is Lemberger, an obscure German variety that yields fresh, strawberryish wine. There is also excellent Syrah grown in one vineyard.

Some of the smallest Washington wineries have made some striking wines in recent years, proving the potential of the grapes from this region. There are more vineyard-designated wines all the time, and subtle differences between each are just beginning to emerge.

The larger Washington wineries can now be regarded as serious, well-established operations – Chateau Ste Michelle, for example, Washington's largest wine producer, owns several state-of-the-art wineries. It also buys forests of oak from which to makes its casks, has invested in new equipment and employs top winemakers to ensure quality from all of its operations. One of its properties, Columbia Crest, is now more or less a separate operation, making a range of good-value wines.

Others of note include Columbia Winery, run by David Lake, the US's only winemaking MW (which is more like a cluster of individual boutiques producing a string of fine wines). And Canoe Ridge Vineyard, a partnership organised by the high-profile Chalone Inc group of California. There are now 85 wineries, most less than two decades old. The pioneer tradition is alive – and kicking.

△ *Harvesting the crop at Columbia Crest, one of Washington's larger wineries and part of Chateau Ste Michelle.*

Oregon

The term 'Pacific Northwest' is more of a stab at a particular reality than an accurate reflection of two very different states – most of the time, it seems as if there's a high wall between Oregon and Washington, sealing off widely varying attitudes, industries, energy levels, outlook and agriculture. While Washington is bustling and slightly brash, Oregon is rather reserved, sedate, decentralised and, above all, earnest. Recycling is a big issue there, environmental concerns loom large, large parts of its city centres are pedestrian-only, and there's no smoking in public buildings or, it often seems, anywhere else. You can still see bumper stickers on cars that read 'Don't Californicate Oregon'. The state was originally settled by farming families who walked nearly 3,280 kilometres to get there on the Oregon Trail. They travelled with quietly stubborn toughness, and they passed it on.

Many of the first settlers saw Oregon as a modern Eden, with good soil, gently rolling hills and a pleasant climate (city dwellers complain about the pervasive winter rain, but few farmers mind it). The state is divided from north to south by the Cascade Mountains, which hold the Pacific rainstorms to the west side; eastern Oregon is a virtual desert, not only dry but subject to extremes of heat and cold. The pioneers followed the rivers and valleys west, and prospered. Today, the majority of the population lives on the west side of the mountains.

One of the favourite pastimes in Oregon is bucking trends. Monoculture looks like the way farming is going in a lot of other places around the world, but not here; there are 200 different crops thriving in Oregon, from hazelnuts to grass seed, peppermint and roses. And when it comes to wine, while the world is stampeding toward Chardonnay and Cabernet Sauvignon, Oregon leans the other way and inclines toward Pinot Noir, Riesling and Pinot Gris.

The strong sense of individuality and idealism also comes through in Oregon's wine-labelling laws, which are the toughest in the US (and even surpass some of

Europe). They stipulate a minimum of 90 per cent of the named grape for any varietal wine, with the exception of Cabernet Sauvignon, which is set at 75 per cent to allow blending with other red Bordeaux varieties. Wines cannot be labelled with generic names taken from other countries, such as 'Champagne' or 'Rhône,' and they must be made entirely from grapes that have been grown in the appellation area. Interestingly, these strict regulations were drawn up by the winemakers, not by the bureaucrats.

The major wine-growing region is the Willamette Valley (pronounced, as they like to say, 'WillAMMit, dammit').This is a huge valley, rivalling San Joaquin in California for size. The appellation, which embraces the hills to the east and west of the Willamette River, goes from the Columbia River a little north of Portland to just south of Eugene, is about 160 kilometres long and 96 kilometres wide at its greatest breadth; most of the wineries and vineyards are, however, clustered in the cooler northern half of the valley. The soils are mostly volcanic, iron-rich, dark brick-red, and the vineyards march up and down rolling hills, a landscape as rumpled as an unmade featherbed, made dramatic by tall stands of fir and pine trees along the ridge lines.

The bulk of production here is of Pinot Noir, and most of the wineries can be found about an hour's drive southwest of Portland in Yamhill County, scattered around what are picturesquely known as 'the Red Hills of Dundee'. Modern Oregon winemaking started a long way south of here, but this is where its present shape was set, in 1965, when David Lett, a young curmudgeon from California, arrived and planted Pinot Noir. It takes a kind of hard-headed romanticism to hitch your wagon to such a temperamental and demanding star as Pinot Noir can be in the vineyard and winery, but Lett was a tireless missionary and good winemaker, and soon had plenty of company.

Many of those first pioneers were career-changers, part-timers and home winemakers intent on turning professional (two of the most distinguished pioneers, David Adelsheim and Dick Ponzi, were, respectively, a banker and an engineer;

△ *Crater Lake, Oregon, highlights the region's volcanic foundations.*

several others were doctors). Some of them made reasonably good wine and are still operating successfully today. Certainly, considerable promise was made manifest from the start.

From the outset few of Oregon's winemakers had much money. Wineries were established in former turkey-processing sheds and fruit-packing or nut-hulling plants, or garages; most of the pioneers didn't quit their day jobs right away, and the wines were often as rustic as their premises, but they got it right enough times to go on. In 1976, in a marathon blind wine tasting of red burgundies in Paris, a US ringer topped the field – 1975 Eyrie Vineyard Pinot Noir, made by David Lett. Outraged, distinguished Burgundian Robert Drouhin staged his own tasting shortly afterwards, and Eyrie did it again.

A couple of reasonable vintages for Pinot Noir helped drum up more interest, and from then on Oregon Pinot Noir began to be taken seriously. Today, it accounts for nearly half of the state's wine production, and is considered Oregon's signature wine. It is, generally, less delicate than the best red burgundy, but usually has the right velvety texture and bright black-cherry fruit that make Pinot Noir so striking and so appealing.

In the 1990s, the pace of the Oregon winemaking industry quickened – plantings began to rise sharply as newcomers arrived. Robert Drouhin was the most notable, and got a hero's welcome. He built a modern, attractive winery called Domaine Drouhin in the hills, surrounded by well-groomed vineyards. More French flavour was added by Champagne firm Laurent-Perrier which also moved in, buying land and planting its own vineyard. Then renowned Australian winemaker Brian Croser founded the Dundee Wine Company, to make sparkling wine and some table wines. Several Californians also moved north, mostly from the Napa Valley. One large winery, Willamette Valley Vineyards, was created with financing by a public stock offering (there are more than 4,000 stockholders), and King Estate, a fairly modern and very grand operation, by a private fortune. Today there are just over 2,800 hectares under vine, about 100 wineries and several well-established négociant

brands, In total approximately 750,000 cases of wine are sold annually, and rusticity is a thing of the past.

The other major regions within Oregon are the Umpqua Valley, just to the south of the Willamette Valley, and the Rogue Valley, further south toward the California border. They are higher and drier and somewhat rockier than the Willamette, and produce wines from a number of varieties. Particularly notable are the admirable, fresh, food-friendly Rieslings and excellent Gewürztraminers. (The northwestern corner of the Willamette Valley, also with higher elevations, has shown some of the same virtues with these varieties.) On the other side of the Cascades, along the Columbia River, the Columbia Valley and Walla Walla Valley appellations are shared with Washington State and account for some decent Gewürztraminer, Riesling, Merlot and Cabernet Sauvignon.

The major white grape variety in terms of vineyard area is Chardonnay, which was planted basically as a commercial necessity but without much enthusiasm from the start. It grows well enough, and sometimes the wine is reasonably good, but not often enough; some expert think the clones are wrong for the soil and climate of this region. Whatever the reason, the wines simply don't inspire, and Chardonnay plantings have levelled off in the last few years.

The rising star now is Pinot Gris, which has always been an attractive wine, and has become a commercial success in Oregon lately – most wineries cannot get enough of it these days. Pinot Gris is grown in all the appellations and performs extremely well, producing characterful, complex wines that are somewhat fruitier than examples from Alsace, and are fuller than Italian Pinot Grigios (a crisp and singular wine).

Oregonians have reached out to fellow Pinot Noir romantics around the world with their International Pinot Noir Festival, gathering in Burgundians, Australians, New Zealanders, Italians, Californians and Chileans to accumulate a large body of knowledge. Pinot Noir being what it is, that's like saying one knows a lot about cats, but it is one more example of a determination they'll see through.

△ *Domaine Drouhin,*
Willamette Valley,
reflects Burgundian
Robert Drouhin's faith
in the region.

New York State

While more grape varieties grow naturally in the US between the Atlantic coast and the Rocky Mountains than in any other place in the world they are, some might say unfortunately, the hearty native labrusca species which produce strong-flavoured wine that most wine drinkers find unappealing. Many of these varieties have high acidity masked by considerable sweetness, and the resulting wines display a characteristic 'foxiness' that has found few fans.

For centuries, enterprising viticulturists tried to raise European vinifera grapes in New York and other eastern states, but they were always defeated by the harsh weather conditions and devastating native vine diseases. French-American hybrid grapes were developed in the 19th century and produced more palatable wines, but frustrated New York winemakers and wine enthusiasts continued to yearn for true European-style wines.

California, with its temperate climate and hospitable environment, has been turning out highly prized wines for over a century, but in the east, the goal remained elusive until the 1970s when, eventually, a host of factors combined to make the vintners' dream a reality. Thanks to technological advancements for combating native vineyard diseases, improved agricultural techniques, refined clonal selection and more controlled practices in the winery, it finally became possible to successfully raise vinifera vines in certain sections of New York State and other eastern US regions.

It's true that most of New York will remain unsuitable for grapes, but four distinct wine producing regions have proven to be hospitable, if challenging, homes for wine grapes: Long Island, the Finger Lakes, Lake Erie and the Hudson River Valley. What makes these particular sites vine-friendly is not just a question of terroir, for each of these places has its own unique soils and weather patterns. The distinctive trait shared by all these regions is that each of them is situated next to a large body of water that moderates their climate.

Long Island

Only an hour or so from New York City, Long Island is surrounded on one side by the Atlantic Ocean and on the other by the waters of the Long Island Sound. Long Island is a 193-kilometre-long bed of gravel, sand and silt left behind by a glacier that slid across the land some 10,000 years ago. The island's well-drained soil and moderate climate are good for vineyards, although none were planted here until 1972 when Louisa and Alex Hargrave planted the first vines.

Today Long Island boasts 16 wineries, most of them located at the far end of the island on the North Fork, a 56-kilometre-long strip of land scarcely eight kilometres wide. Only vinifera grapes are grown on Long Island. Chardonnay has long been the most successful Long Island wine, but promising Cabernet Franc, Merlot and Cabernet Sauvignon are also beginning to be produced here.

The Finger Lakes

Virtually all the Finger Lakes vineyards are planted close to the shores of three large, deep lakes: Cayuga, Keuka, and Seneca. Aggressively flavoured sweet wines from native American grapes were the norm here until 1953, when Dr Konstantin Frank, a Russian emigré, successfully raised Riesling and other vinifera grapes.

Today, approximately 50 per cent of Finger Lakes grapes are labrusca varieties (especially Catawba, Niagara, Delaware) and French-American hybrids (notably Seyval, Vidal Blanc, Cayuga, Chamourcin, Baco Noir and Marechal Foche). The newest and most enterprising vintners, however, are focusing exclusively on vinifera grape varieties, especially the popular Pinot Noir, Cabernet Franc, Cabernet Sauvignon and Merlot, not to mention Riesling from the Finger Lakes, which is among the best in the US.

Lake Erie

The unique, narrow plateau of gravel and loam left along the shores of Lake Erie by retreating glaciers resembles the soils of coastal regions. The climate is tempered by warmth reflected from the lake. In the 19th century Lake Erie was an important wine centre, but the industry here never quite recovered from Prohibition. Most of the wines are still traditional, often sweet wines made from labrusca and hybrid grapes (Catawba, Niagara, Delaware, Seyval, Vidal, Cayuga, Baco Noir, Chambourcin and Marechal Foche.) A few pioneers are beginning to introduce vinifera vines.

The Hudson River

The Hudson River Valley is the oldest grape-growing region in the US, founded by the French Huguenots who planted table grapes when they arrived in the 1670s and found that vinifera could not survive. In 1977 several hybrids, most notably the Duchess, were developed here, leading to the first ventures in commercial winemaking. Prohibition brought the industry to a temporary halt, but it was revived by Mark Miller, who founded Benmarl Vineyards in the 1960s.

△ *Lenz Winery, North Fork, Long Island, is one of the best in the region and produces fine Chardonnay.*

Canada

Although there are 100 hectares of vine struggling to survive in ice-bound Quebec, and a little winemaking takes place in Nova Scotia, Canada's wine industry is based almost entirely in two provinces, British Columbia and Ontario. Even here wine-making has only just come of age. Canada's wine used to be so poor that as recently as the late 1970s, it was mandatory for restaurants in British Columbia seeking a liquor licence to list at least two regional wines on the list. At least that way a few people tried it just the once.

Times have changed for the better since then. A new generation of serious and dynamic winemakers from both regions has spent the late 20th century upgrading the vineyards and the wineries, putting quality before quantity. And, while there is still a long way to go, their efforts are gradually paying off.

Although both British Columbia and Ontario have grown grapes for wine since the 1860s, Canada's vineyards were, until recently, dominated by hardy non-vinifera or hybrid varieties, the only vines believed to survive the country's extremely harsh winters. The oldest vinifera vines date from 1963, but premium Canadian wine was not truly taken seriously until the 1980s, when the Vintners Quality Alliance (VQA), an appellation of origin system, was set up in Ontario. It was during this decade that grape-growers started grubbing up many of the second-rate vines and replacing them with such internationally desirable grapes as Chardonnay, Cabernet Sauvignon and Merlot.

In the midst of such wholescale change, the Canadian wine industry has had the good sense to hang on to the one style for which it is highly acclaimed, Icewine. Intense and opulent dessert wines made from the concentrated juice of frozen berries, Icewines are produced in both regions, usually from Riesling, Chardonnay or the one hybrid that is still approved, Vidal. Canada makes more Icewine than any other country in the world, and each year bags yet more international awards for it.

British Columbia

With just over 1,000 hectares, British Columbia has one-tenth of Ontario's vineyard land. The local winemakers describe their task as 'frontier grape-growing', as they battle with their northern desert region of sandy soils, arid summers and fiercely cold winters. Having said that, the prime vineyard sites around Lake Okanagan are relatively temperate and lush. Lake Okanagan lies one hour's flight inland from Vancouver, a 145-kilometre-long strip of water and green valley slopes in the middle of vast folds of dusty mountain. At the cool northern end of the Okanagan Valley, aromatic whites such as Riesling, Pinot Gris, Gewürztraminer and local speciality Ehrenfelser (a Riesling/Silvaner cross) hold sway, although some patches are gradually being replanted with Chardonnay. Pinot Blanc is a speciality, often sold in Vancouver restaurants as the classic partner for Pacific salmon dishes.

Further south, beyond the lake, rattlesnakes and scorpions scuttle through the vines in an area so hot and arid that winemakers have dubbed it 'The Beach' – nonetheless, this is where red grape varieties, and particularly Merlot, are beginning to show most promise.

Ontario

Ontario's wine country is truly picturesque, from the historic rural community of Pelee Island in Lake Erie, to the Niagara Peninsula vineyards, protected from the extremes of a continental climate by air circulating between Lake Ontario and the high Niagara escarpment. Around 40 wineries work 550 vineyard sites in the province, making nearly three times as much wine as in British Columbia. The climate is relatively cool throughout, the vineyard soils varied.

Ontario concentrates mainly on white wines (Chardonnay, Pinot Blanc, Gewürz-traminer, Riesling, Vidal). Reds include Pinot Noir, Gamay, Merlot and Cabernets Sauvignon and Franc. The aromatic white varieties are slowly giving way to more Chardonnay and the reds lag behind in quality, although there are honourable exceptions. Icewine and late-harvest wines are as important here as in BC.

△ *Vines mix with fir trees along the shores of Vaseux Lake, British Columbia.*

Recommended Producers

California

Carneros

Acacia Winery – Fairly typical Carneros success story – young winemakers with high ideals, grape-grower partners, unglamorous and functional winery, all adding up to fine Pinot Noirs and Chardonnays, either from single vineyards or blended.

Cline Cellars – The Cline family started as grape-growers who got into winemaking in a rough-and-ready way, but their grape varieties happened to be Rhône types. In on the ground floor of the 'Rhône Renaissance', the Clines have thrived, with a new winery and vineyards in Carneros.

Saintsbury – David Graves and Richard Ward have been making outstanding Chardonnay and Pinot Noir since the early 1980s. Their wines have become the benchmarks for the Carneros style, bursting with character but perfectly balanced.

Napa Valley

Beaulieu Vineyards – One of California's oldest and most distinguished wineries, especially known for Cabernet Sauvignon (George de Latour Private Reserve is top of the range). The careful, classic house style has, wavered under corporate ownership recently.

Beringer Vineyards – Founded in 1876, Beringer has been a top winery and has also scraped bottom during its history. Intelligently overhauled in the 1970s by new corporate owners and in the hands of a good winemaking team, it has gone from strength to strength. Excellent, serious examples of Merlot, Cabernet Sauvignon and, especially, Chardonnay.

Clos du Val – Bernard Portet is French to his fingertips, born and bred in Bordeaux, but he has made his fame as a pioneer of both the Stag's Leap District and Carneros. Here he produces outstanding Cabernet Sauvignon and Merlot, fine Pinot Noir and notably muscular Zinfandel.

Franciscan Vineyards – This low-profile winery is quietly establishing itself as a consistent producer of stylish, straightforward wines at reasonable prices (usually, in fact, bargains). Seek out the fine Merlot, Chardonnay and Zinfandel.

Frog's Leap – A long-standing partnership between John Williams and Larry Turley resulted in some of California's top Sauvignon Blancs and excellent Zinfandels; now winemaker Williams is operating on his own here, still doing well with those two varieties, as well as a first-rate Merlot.

Heitz Wine Cellars – Joe Heitz is one of the mainstays of the modern era in the Napa Valley, famous for blunt speech and idiosyncrasy, as well as powerful, acclaimed Cabernet Sauvignons, especially the singular Martha's Vineyard.

Robert Mondavi Winery – One of the most famous winemakers in the world, Bob Mondavi is a restless, innovative, missionary of wine and the good life. He created the distinctive style Fumé Blanc and gave it its name, made some of the first oak-aged wines in California, and pioneered cold fermentation and unfiltered wines. His Cabernet and Pinot Noir are often outstanding, Fumé Blanc and Chardonnay among the best. There is also a second label for his wines made in the Lodi area; these are known as Robert Mondavi Woodbridge and are examples of well-made mass-market wines.

Mumm Napa Valley – A consistently good sparkling-wine producer, connected with the French Champagne house; thanks to extensive prime vineyards in Carneros and the southern Napa Valley.

Opus One – Bold, lavish, expensive – and that's just the building! The joint venture of Robert Mondavi and Château Mouton-Rothschild incorporated one of Mondavi's prime vineyards and the expertise of both wineries to make a superb Cabernet blend.

Schramsberg – Here, Jack Davies created stylish, consistent, vintage-dated sparkling wines made from classic grape varieties 30 years ago and was the leading producer for decades. In a now-crowded field, Schramsberg still stands out.

Shafer Vineyards – Overlooking the sought-after Stag's Leap District, Shafer proves many of the clichés about good wines coming from hillsides, with poor soil and plenty of sunlight. Talent and dedication help: the Merlot and Cabernet Sauvignon from here are truly fine.

Stag's Leap Wine Cellars – The winery that won the infamous Paris tasting of 1976 and put California on the world's premium-wine map has mellowed nicely. Cabernets are still long-lived and rich (there are several, from different vineyards), well worth seeking out.

Sonoma

Dry Creek Vineyards – Dave Stare's winery sits in the middle of what is now a thriving viticultural area, but in the early 1970s the Dry Creek Valley was a lonely place for such a pioneer. He made his name with steely Fumé Blanc, then followed this with fine Cabernet Sauvignon.

E&J Gallo – This, the world's largest winery, is well-known for mass-market, clean, sound and understated wines. It is now the leading vineyard owner in Sonoma County and has embarked on an upgrade programme of premium wines. Results so far have been mixed, but anything can happen.

Jordan – Once the most expensive winery built in California, Jordan raised expectations it has never quite fulfilled, even though several vintages of Cabernet Sauvignon have been marvellous. Now also produces 'J,' a first-rate sparkling wine.

Kenwood Vineyards – Begun in 1970 as a family enterprise making rustic reds in a plain wooden building, Kenwood is now a medium-sized, sophisticated winemaking facility, still family-run. Outstanding Zinfandel, Cabernet, Sauvignon Blanc.

Matanzas Creek – Off by itself in a corner of Sonoma increasingly being eaten into by expanding suburbs, this winery quietly rolls out serious, fine Merlot, Sauvignon Blanc and Chardonnay.

Simi Winery – Zelma Long was known as America's leading female winemaker when she took over here; now, she's known simply as one of America's very best winemakers. Of quite a few wines, her Chardonnay and Cabernet stand out.

Williams Selyem – Ed Selyem and Burt Williams are two down-to-earth, plain-spoken guys who once made some of the best Pinot Noir in California in a converted garage. Now they are in a proper winery, but have not let that spoil them. Their output is tiny, but well worth seeking out.

Mendocino

Fetzer Vineyards – An extraordinary success story: small vineyard becomes family winery, expands rapidly, Dad dies, children press on with expansion, reach multi-million case level, organic grape-growing programme begins, kids get a bit tired and sell the winery for a reputed fortune. The happy ending seems ongoing, as the corporate owners are upholding quality standards for a wide range of wines.

McDowell Valley Vineyards – It's solar-powered, it's remote, and it has had a wobbly history – in its early days the winery reacted, rather uncertainly, to trends. But the vineyard is good, and now McDowell Valley is on course as a Rhône-style producer. Luscious Syrah and Viognier.

Central Coast

Bonny Doon – An eccentric character, but serious winemaker, Randall Grahm is best known for his well-made Rhône-style wines, but is actually a restless tinkerer with a fondness for neglected varieties. His Italian-style wines come from a property known as Ca' del Solo in Monterey.

Calera Wine Company – Josh Jensen is a Burgundian at heart – he never takes the easy way. His tiny, low-technology winery sits in the remote, rugged limestone hills of the Gavilan Mountains, where he makes quirky, rich and powerful Pinot Noir.

Chalone – Atop a mountain overlooking Monterey, Chalone has been likened to a monastery – they had no water or electricity for more than a decade. The wines, of course, are Burgundian, mostly dense and oaky Pinot Noir and Chardonnay.

Ridge Vineyards – The last survivors of a once-great area (Santa Clara, above Silicon Valley) uphold the standard with one of California's great Cabernets, known as Monte Bello. Perhaps better known for brawny, sensuous, long-lived Zinfandels made from vineyards all over California.

Santa Barbara

Au Bon Climat – Flamboyant character Jim Clendenen makes small, single-vineyard batches of splendid, long-lived Chardonnays and robust Pinot Noirs in various styles.

RECOMMENDED PRODUCERS

△ *The legendary Robert Mondavi of Napa, creator of the popular white wine style Fumé Blanc and also co-proprietor of Opus One Winery.*

Firestone Vineyard – Brooks Firestone, of the tyre family, is energetic and a believer in positive thinking. The winery once made lovely Riesling and Gewürztraminer as those wines were going out of fashion, now emphasises easy-going Merlot and Bordeaux-style blends.

Qupé – Bob Lindquist is part of the group that was responsible for Au Bon Climat and several other offbeat Santa Barbara enterprises – he is the Rhône offshoot, making sensational Syrahs from different vineyards, and exceptional Viognier.

Washington

Canoe Ridge Vineyard – Major partners in this new venture are Chalone, Inc., owners of Chalone winery in California and involved in partnerships in other properties. The vineyard overlooks the Columbia River, in an established viticultural area; Chardonnay and Merlot are the focus.

Chateau Ste Michelle – This is a large winery that has diversified and maintained a high quality level as it has grown, becoming the driving force in Washington winemaking over the last two decades. It consists of several thousand acres of vineyards and three separate wineries, with carefully separate functions. Lately, more wines are vineyard-designated. Produces several consistently good Cabernet Sauvignons and excellent Merlot.

Columbia Crest – A spin-off brand of Chateau Ste Michelle, now operates as separate brand altogether, offering relatively low-priced, very good-value Chardonnay, Cabernet Sauvignon and Merlot.

Columbia Winery – The pioneering Washington winery, originally the semi-professional hobby of a group of university professors. Now run by David Lake, a Canadian who gained his Master of Wine certificate in England, it is a medium-sized, thoroughly sophisticated operation, producing outstanding Sémillon, Merlot, vineyard-designated Cabernets and a luscious Syrah.

Covey Run – Run by several partners who own vineyards, the winery has often had a problem with consistency – some wines have been excellent, most of them are rather straightforward and ordinary. However, overall the output continues to be promising.

Hogue Cellars – A low-key operation run as part of a large farming enterprise, Hogue produces solid, reliable wines with firm, forward flavours, especially Fumé Blanc, Sémillon, Merlot and Cabernet Sauvignon.

Woodward Canyon – Award-winning wines are made in small quantities here, mostly with the emphasis on Chardonnay and Cabernet Sauvignon with a tendency to strong oak flavour.

Oregon

Adelsheim Vineyards – Handsome, winsome drawings adorn the wine labels here, conveying the idea of a small family winery hand-crafting stylish wines. Dave Adelsheim fled the banking business for this, and the elegant Pinot Noirs and Pinot Gris prove it is a labour of love.

Archery Summit – Gary and Nancy Andrus came from the Napa Valley in search of some simpler winemaking pleasures, and found them with straightforward, well-textured Pinot Noir.

Benton Lane – More Napa expats, this time Steve Girard and Carl Doumani; the first releases of Pinot Noir have been solid, meaty wines of some distinction.

Domaine Drouhin – When the well-known and long-established wine firm from Burgundy set up shop in the Willamette Valley, the locals were flattered and awed. Though there were some sceptics, they've subsequently been converted by a string of rich, lightly spicy Pinot Noirs that are among Oregon's best.

Elk Cove Vineyards – After a somewhat uneven start as a part-time venture, Elk Cove has settled down to more consistent success with several full-bodied Pinot Noirs and crisp Pinot Gris and Riesling.

King Estate Winery – The King family burst onto the Oregon wine scene in the early 1990s, buying a 550-acre hillside estate, planting most of it as vineyard, setting up a root stock nursery, and building an ultramodern winery. Bought-in grapes were made into stylish wines (Pinot Noir, Pinot Gris, Chardonnay), and the subsequent estate wines were fine. The family is ambitious, idealistic, and well-financed – stay tuned.

Knudsen-Erath – Dick Erath was one of the early refugees from California and has always had a knack for balanced, medium-bodied Pinot Noirs from several vineyards, almost like chapters in an Oregon Pinot Noir textbook over the years. Also makes an easy-going Riesling.

Montinore Vineyards – A grand old mansion presides over this large vineyard estate in northern Oregon, planted to several varieties of grapes. Early efforts were perhaps over-ambitious and diverse, and sometimes still are. Pinot Noir and Pinot Gris are good, standard-issue versions, improved enough to show further possibilities of improvement.

Ponzi Vineyards – Dick Ponzi is one of Oregon's winemaking pioneers, combining a restless, driving curiosity with hard work and good humour (his personalised licence plate reads 'capo,' Italian for 'chief,' and he sometimes recommends his Pinot Noir as a match for pizza). Deep, complex Pinot Noir, dry and tight Alsatian-style Pinot Gris and Riesling.

Rex Hill Vineyards – The architecturally striking wooden winery building is actually a renovated fruit-drying shed; inside, the ornate tasting room belies the seriousness of the winemaking. As many as five or six good-to-fine Pinot Noirs are released every year, mostly vineyard-designated, as well as a reasonable example of Pinot Gris.

Willamette Valley Vineyards – This winery was established by way of a public stock offering. It's large, beautiful, and perched on a hillside with spectacular views and the tasting room does a lively business. There is a bewildering array of wines, some rather frivolous. Lately, the Pinot Noir and Pinot Gris have been better than expected.

New York State

Long Island

Bedell Cellars – Considered by many to be Long Island's best winery, Bedell produces Chardonnay, Cygnet (a blend of Riesling and Gewürztraminer) Merlot, Cabernet Sauvignon, Main Road Red (a Merlot/

Cabernet blend) and Eis, a Riesling dessert wine. Winemaker-owner Kip Bedell owns 30 acres of vines and produces 8,000 cases of wine annually.

Duckwalk – One of two wineries on South Fork, though most grapes come from North Fork. Owned by Pindar.

Gristina Vineyards – Founded by the Gristina family in 1983, this firm makes good Chardonnay, Merlot, Cabernet Sauvignon and some of Long Island's best Pinot Noir.

Hargrave Vineyard – The region's first commercial wine producer and much expanded since those early days; Louisa and Alex Hargrave are particularly known for their Chardonnay and Pinot Noir. Hargrave Reserve wines are much admired.

Lenz Winery – Look for well rounded Chardonnay, Cabernet and, occasionally, Pinot Noir. Crisp sparkling wines and a fragrant Pinot Blanc are recent additions.

Osprey's Dominion – After a few troubled years, Osprey's is up and running again, producing respectable reds. One unusual advantage here is that Osprey's owns an old, established vineyard.

Palmer Vineyards – One of the largest and most successful New York wineries, Palmer produces a full range of wines including examples of Chardonnay, Sauvignon Blanc and Cabernet Franc.

Paumanock Vineyards – Owner-winemaker Charles Massoud began planting his vines in 1983. He makes Chardonnays, Rieslings, a range of reds and, when climatic conditions are right, a terrific, rich late-harvest Chenin Blanc.

Pellegrini Vineyards – One of Long Island's finest producers. Try the lush Chardonnay, the Cabernet, the Merlot and the late harvest Gewürztraminer.

Pindar Vineyards – With 400 acres and producing well over 50,000 cases of wine, this is Long Island's largest winery, with 14 different wines, from Chardonnay to a sparkling Pinot Meunier.

Sagpond Vineyards – Located on the South Fork, this relative newcomer's strength is Chardonnay, with Cabernet and Merlot looking good for the future. Brand new US$2 million tasting room just opened.

△ Zelma Long, one of the top winemakers in the US and the driving force behind Simi winery.

The Finger Lakes

Fox Run Vineyards – New owner Scott Osborn and winemaker Peter Bell have begun turning out some of the region's most promising wines, including Chardonnay, Riesling, Merlot and Cabernet Franc.

Glenora – Particularly known for fine sparkling wines, Glenora also makes good Chardonnay and Riesling.

Lamoreaux Landing Wine Cellars – Perhaps the most exciting winery in the Finger Lakes; top-notch Chardonnay, Riesling and Pinot Noir are made in a stunning facility.

Standing Stone Vineyards – Founded in 1993, this newcomer has already gathered numerous awards for its Riesling and Gewürztraminer. The Cabernet Franc and Merlot look promising.

Hermann J Wiemer Vineyard – Hermann Wiemer has been making wines in the Finger Lakes since the 1970s. His Rieslings can resemble fine German wines.

Dr Frank's Vinifera Wine Cellars – The first Finger Lakes winery to produce vinifera wines, Dr Frank's is now run by the late founder's son, Willy Frank. It still turns out some of the best Riesling, Gewürztraminer and Pinot Noir in the region.

The Hudson River Valley

Benmarl – The first contemporary winery in the Hudson region, Brenmarl produces a range of wines mostly from hybrid grapes. There is a spectacular view of the Hudson from the hillside vineyards.

Cascade Mountain Winery – Founded 1977, Cascade has improved over the last couple of years with drier, more sophisticated wines. Most are hybrids, sometimes blended with vinifera. Note the nice little restaurant in the tasting room.

Clinton Vineyards – The only wine made here is a mere 1,800 cases of crisp, fruity Seyval Blanc.

Millbrook Vineyard & Winery – One of the best and most innovative wineries in New York. Owned by John Dyson, former NY State Commissioner of Agriculture. Look for Chardonnay, Cabernet and Sangiovese. Some wines are made from grapes provided by vineyards in California owned by Dyson.

Canada

British Columbia

Gray Monk – BC's best exponent of aromatic whites, and a long-established family operation. George Sr and sons Stephen and George Jr remain loyal to their Riesling, Pinot Gris and Auxerrois plantings, although their wide portfolio also includes fair Chardonnay, several reds and delicious dessert wines.

Mission Hill – An ambitious and progressive operation which has set out to make an impact internationally, Mission Hill caused a stir in 1992 when it persuaded New Zealand's John Simes, formerly chief winemaker at Montana, to head up its team. Since then the wines has gone from strength to strength, with the Mission Hill Chardonnay consistently one of BC's best.

Quails' Gate Estate – One of the oldest producing vineyard sites in the Okanagan valley, Quails' Gate is now thoroughly up-to-date, with Croser-trained Australian winemaker Jeff Martin at the helm turning out fulsome, complex Chardonnay and a set of rich reds which show what can be achieved with Pinot Noir in particular.

Sumac Ridge – Harry McWatters, chairman of the local wine institute, marshalls his large team into producing a full range of styles, including enjoyable Pinot Blanc, Chardonnay and a decent sparkling wine (made using a high proportion of Pinot Blanc). A sound range of reds show the progress being made with new vineyards in the hot southern 'Beach' area.

Summerhill Estate – Sparkling wines with crisp and pure fruit flavours – the result of strict organic policies, or new-age guru Stephen Cipes' belief in the energy-giving properties of ageing wine in pyramids? Off the wall, perhaps, but the high quality results are impressive.

Ontario

Cave Springs – Founded in 1986 with the intention of using grapes exclusively from the high escarpment close to Lake Ontario, which Angelo Pavan and Robert Summers believe to provide one of Ontario's most promising micro-climates. The wide range

proves their point, especially the excellent
Chardonnay.

Chateau des Charmes – Paul Michel Bosc,
a fifth-generation French wine-grower who
came to Canada in the 1960s, consistently
produces some of Ontario's most impressive
whites, especially Chardonnays, while his
reds, made from Pinot Noir, Cabernet
Sauvignon and Gamay, aren't bad either.
A classy outfit making the most of Niagara
Peninsula fruit.

Henry of Pelham – Small winery located
on the Niagara Bench escarpment with a
75-acre estate, producing a range in which
soft, ripe Chardonnay stands out. The
whites are more impressive than the reds.

Inniskillin – One of the first Niagara
wineries to make an impact outside Canada,
Inniskillin was established by flamboyant
entrepreneur Donald Ziraldo and
introspective perfectionist Karl Kaiser in
1974. Most of the international plaudits go
to the superbly crafted Icewines, or the
whites – Chardonnay, Riesling, Pinot Gris.
Reds are also made in limited quantities.

Pelee Island Winery – Walter Schmoranz
makes wine on the rectangular scrap of land
out in the middle of Lake Erie between the
shores of Canada and the US. Schmoranz,
an articulate and extrovert character, was
trained in the Rheingau, and produces
elegant aromatic whites, a soft, strawberry-
scented Pinot Noir and a juicy
Gamay/Zweigelt blend.

Southbrook Farms – Originally a fruit and
vegetable farm, Southbrook began to make
wines officially in the early 1990s. Already
a peppery Auxerrois, toasty Chardonnay
and blackberry-flavoured Cabernet Franc
stand out, although Southbrook Farms is
still best known for its elixir-like fruit
liqueurs (framboise and cassis).

△ *David Lett has been
making excellent wines
in Willamette, Oregon,
since 1965. His white
wines are said to
resemble burgundy.*

South America

A NEW WORLD ENGINE WITH AN OLD WORLD LOG BOOK is a fair way of describing the 'southern cone' of South America's wine machine. Vines were brought down from Mexico by missionaries in the mid-16th century, with wine being made in order to celebrate the Eucharist. The tradition was carried on by the *conquistadores* who preferred local wine to the travel-sick drink parcels sent over from Spain. Add to that the subsequent vine planting by European immigrants over the last century, and you have a long and multi-layered backbone to the wine industry. Today, the 20th century version of the conquistadores are the flying winemakers, bringing new ideas and techniques to the continent. From the Rio Grande do Sol in Brazil, through Uruguay's Rivera region, Mendoza in Argentina, to the lush vineyards of Chile and up to the Ica valley of Peru, latent potential is being turned into exciting flavours. It's not just the speed of discovery and the pace of change that induces gaping-jaw syndrome, it's the thought of what is still to come.

▽ *Vineyards in Chile's Casablanca Valley, where sea mists help to produce quality wine in a dry region.*

Chile

Nowhere is this physical potential greater than in Chile's Central Valley, where phylloxera-free vines enjoy the monotony of virtually zero vintage variation. Between November and March there is no rain, and the combination of hot, dry days, and cold nights allows long, gradual maturation. Growing grapes is as easy as spotting mountains in Chile, but making quality wine has proved to be much more of a struggle.

Like a talented teenager that can't be bothered to use what he's got, Chile blundered through the 1970s and most of the 1980s, making tired, oxidised wines that the local market lapped up. Then, prompted by visionaries like Miguel Torres,

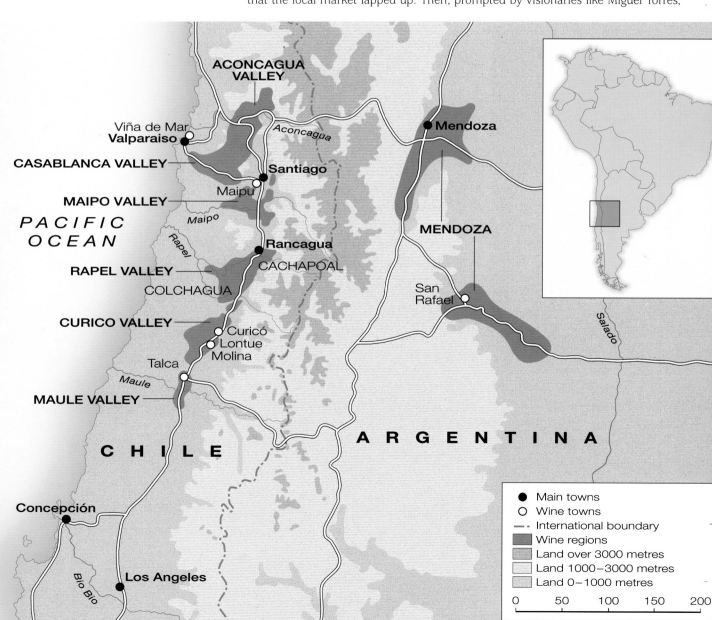

there followed an investment phase, which generated the false belief that good wine is made in shiny, expensive wineries. Old *rauli* (the native 'beech') barrels were burnt, stainless steel replaced concrete; and although quality went up a notch, it was really just a false dawn to the modern era. Only in the last two years has the industry 'returned to the roots' with the realisation that progress will only come with improvement in the quality of fruit coming into those wineries.

Back in the vineyards, decades of neglect along with cycles of rip-it-up, replant, then tear-it-up-again, had left a picture of varietal muddling and badly-tended vines. Suddenly, concepts like vineyard mapping, canopy management and controlled irrigation were, and are, being grasped firmly. And, with better quality rootstock and lower yields, the raw materials being harvested are now almost unrecognisable.

At the same time, Chilean winemakers who for decades have been stifled by insular attitudes and channelled by a history of French influence, are travelling more, experimenting more, and taking a few more risks in their attempt to make classic wines. Extended skin contact, wild yeast fermentation, no filtration – this is the blueprint for premium projects being pinned on winery walls.

Cabernet Sauvignon and the Bordeaux blends of the Maipo were the wines that launched Chile, but other varieties from 'emerging' regions are at the forefront of today's revolution. Chardonnay and Sauvignon Blanc from Casablanca, Pinot Noir from Chimbarongo, and Merlot from Cachapoal; these are the combinations to watch. And despite delays caused by strict quarantine laws, the influx of Italian and Rhône varietals is gathering pace.

Variety is something the Chilean wine portfolio desperately needs, and the question remains as to whether any pattern of regional wine styles will emerge now that new appellation laws are in place. At present, only Casablanca wines stand out from the pack, with their clean definition and strong varietal character. Elsewhere, the boundaries are more blurred, and you are more likely to find differences by picking out wines in an east to west line within individual regions.

Until this period of frenetic change settles down and some sort of regional hierarchy is allowed to emerge, it is better to follow the winemaker rather than the location. Already, Chile's 50-odd exporting wineries are splitting into two main groups; those that are just along for the ride, and those that are using the boom to extend the boom. It is these pioneers and innovators that will ensure Chile is still generating the most noise at the New World millenium party.

Aconcagua Valley

Dominated by vineyards of table grapes, the hot, dry Aconcagua valley contains only one major winery, Errázuriz Estates. When Don Maximiano Errázuriz Valdivieso started planting 100 kilometres northeast of Santiago in 1870, he was probably laughed out of the wine society. But, the land that was considered 'unpromising' turned out to be perfect for vines, and at one stage the property grew to 1,000 hectares. Loamy, clay soils with slow permeability allow good drainage, the Aconcagua river supplies water for irrigation, and daily coastal breezes lower temperatures that are generally higher than the Maipo. Another key factor is the high

△ *Canopy management has revolutionised vine growing in Chile – here grapes are harvested in the Rapel Valley.*

luminosity in this area with an average of 270 clear days a year allowing good rates of photosynthesis. The number of hectares of vineyard has shrunk radically, but Errazuriz's Don Maximiano estate – planted exclusively to Cabernet Sauvignon – continues to produce one of Chile's best premium reds. Using low yield fruit, extended maceration, and up to 20 months in new French oak, the wine is intense and spicy, with tougher tannins than normally found in Chilean reds and a structure to withstand at least eight years bottle ageing. Apart from the Casablanca Valley (see below), the only other subregion of Aconcagua is Panquehue, situated on a flat plain between the towns of Llay-Llay and San Felipe.

Casablanca Valley

Ten years ago, there were more cows than vines in Casablanca. Today, this cool coastal valley is at the forefront of Chile's white wine revolution, and unless the world's wine drinkers revert to milk, dairy farming will never return. Born out of one man's quest to find a 'Chilean Carneros', Casablanca Valley and its easily identifiable wine style has provided a focus for regionality (in a country desperately searching for style diversity) and a kick of self-belief for Chile's winemakers whose white wine portfolio previously lacked a world class personality.

So, why is the quality so good? Lying only 40 kilometres from the port of Valparaiso, the 16 kilometre-long infertile valley is influenced by a maritime climate, delivering daily cooling breezes to take the sting out of summer heat and help extend the growing season. The direct result is a harvest lag of up to two weeks behind the rest of the Central Valley, greater concentration of fruit and firmer natural acidity, with a recognisable citrus edge to the Chardonnay fruit. But microclimate is not the sole factor influencing Casablanca's rapid rise. When Pablo Morande planted his 20 hectares of Chardonnay, Sauvignon Blanc and Riesling in 1982, he started with a clean slate. There was no wine history to follow, no traditional vineyard practices to challenge, and he and the stampede that followed in the planting boom of 1989 to 1990 could start with the best vines and experiment with canopy management.

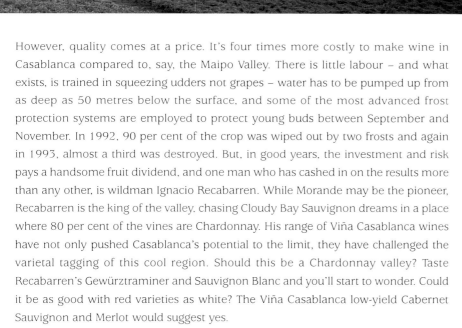

However, quality comes at a price. It's four times more costly to make wine in Casablanca compared to, say, the Maipo Valley. There is little labour – and what exists, is trained in squeezing udders not grapes – water has to be pumped up from as deep as 50 metres below the surface, and some of the most advanced frost protection systems are employed to protect young buds between September and November. In 1992, 90 per cent of the crop was wiped out by two frosts and again in 1993, almost a third was destroyed. But, in good years, the investment and risk pays a handsome fruit dividend, and one man who has cashed in on the results more than any other, is wildman Ignacio Recabarren. While Morande may be the pioneer, Recabarren is the king of the valley, chasing Cloudy Bay Sauvignon dreams in a place where 80 per cent of the vines are Chardonnay. His range of Viña Casablanca wines have not only pushed Casablanca's potential to the limit, they have challenged the varietal tagging of this cool region. Should this be a Chardonnay valley? Taste Recabarren's Gewürztraminer and Sauvignon Blanc and you'll start to wonder. Could it be as good with red varieties as white? The Viña Casablanca low-yield Cabernet Sauvignon and Merlot would suggest yes.

There's not much more room for planting in Casablanca. It's too expensive to pump water up to the valley slopes, so the 1,400 hectares of vines is unlikely to increase. What will arrive soon, though, are wineries. Up until now, only Champagne Mumm has built a facility, and when the rest of the valley's wines are at last made in situ, we can expect a huge jump in quality.

Maipo Valley

The Maipo Valley's dominance in Chilean wine history has more to do with luck than superior physical attributes. Its proximity to the capital Santiago meant that when copper-rich landowners of the 19th century decided to showcase their wealth with vineyards, the Maipo was the most accessible shop window. Although Claudio Gay had set up an experimental nursery in the 1830s, the valley's true founding father was Don Silvestre Ochagavia Echazarreta. He shipped a variety of French vine

△ *Sunrise in the historic vineyards of Viña Errázuriz, north of Santiago in the Aconcagua Valley.*

cuttings to Chile in 1851, just before phylloxera hit Europe, thus ensuring a store of unplagued rootstock and a unique marketing edge for future generations. Families like the Cousiños, Concha y Toros and Undurragas followed Ochagavia's lead, and with a healthy supply of French winemakers (forced into exile by bug-induced unemployment), the Maipo's viticultural roots took shape.

Despite still being dominated by the old giants of the wine industry, there has been enough new activity to suggest that faith in this valley is not just being held up by historical inertia. Frenchmen Bruno Prats and Paul Pontallier decided it was worth risking the advancing smog to test their Cabernet skills close to Santiago, Burgundy's William Fèvre is conjuring Chardonnay tricks high up in the Andean foothills, and investigative sniffing for vineyard sites in the coastal area around San Antonio is more than just tentative.

With all Chilean wine regions, the most important physical influences are the mountains and rivers. In particular, the distance relative to the Andean and coastal ranges dictates the balance between cold nightly downdrafts off the former, and cool breezes circulating the latter. The Pacific-bound Maipo river runs east to west, and has a large effect on the soils. Vineyards close to the Maipo tend to be stonier and higher in salts, while those further away are sandier. However, the concept of terroir has not filtered easily into the psyche of the Chilean wine industry, and only in the last two years has serious vineyard mapping taken place in the Maipo.

A taste tour across the valley reveals the Maipo's dominant varietal and trump card – Cabernet Sauvignon – in a large number of guises. Close to the Andes the Cabernets tend to have more delicate aromatics and elegant structures. Further down the valley near Buin, grapes can be harvested up to 15 days later and wines lean more towards power than subtlety. Finally, to the west, where the Maipo's floodplain spreads out and coastal breezes temper midday heat, simplicity and clarity of fruit are the common denominators.

A list of the great Cabernet blends of the Maipo reads like a 'Who's Who' of Chile's top red wines: Antiguas Reservas, Casa Real, Magnificum, Don Melchor,

Finnis Terra. All have the structure to age, but suppleness that allows early drinking. Chardonnay is the main white grape in the Maipo and performs best at higher altitudes and on sites where the river has washed down calcium from the Andes. Good examples come from Santa Carolina's Santa Rosa estate (on the edge of the Pre-Cordillera), and the predominant style is much weightier and more tropical than a Casablanca model.

The Maipo's future will undoubtedly be dictated by the spread of the capital city overshadowing it. There is certain to be confrontation between winemakers' belief in the irreplaceable fruit of this valley, and the peso-conscious bosses who will be led by the financial logic of moving south.

Rapel Valley

Ten years ago, if you turned east off the PanAmerican Highway just south of San Fernando and headed towards the surfers' paradise of Pichilemu, you would have seen vineyards either side of the road but virtually no wineries. Today, the same trip would undoubtedly be delayed by trucks carrying stainless steel tanks, pneumatic presses and oak barrels. From being a supplier of grapes to the major wineries in the Maipo, the Rapel Valley has suddenly come alive with the buzz of boutique wineries, keeping the fruit in the region, and putting Rapel onto the viticultural map. This is the valley chosen by top winemaker Pablo Morande to launch his US$15 million winemaking project, Viña Morande, whose winery is being built near Pelequen.

Rapel extends between the town of Rancagua in the north to Chimbarongo in the south, and is divided into two main zones; the Cachapoal and Colchagua valleys. Criss-crossed by tributary rivers and transverse ranges of mountains, the area has a rich resource of microclimates that the small wineries have exploited. Of over 8,000 hectares planted throughout the Rapel valley, over 5,000 hectares are red varieties, with Merlot and Cabernet Sauvignon being the dominant grapes.

The Cachapoal valley is home to some of the Central Valley's largest fruit farms, thanks to the rich clay soils; soils that Merlot has settled into particularly well. There

△ *Stainless steel technology in action at the Carmen winery in the hot inland section of the southern Maipo Valley.*

are far fewer wineries than in the crowded Colchagua, and most of the fruit is trucked out by Concha y Toro and Santa Rita. However, Viña La Rosa and Viña Gracia are producing stunning results from vineyards around Peumo and Totihue.

Further south in the Colchagua valley names like Casa Lapostolle, Mont Gras and Luis Felipe Edwards are raising the reputation of the region with their first vintages. Summer temperatures tend to be higher than in the Maipo but strong southwesterly winds between January and March keep the mercury under 30°C. In addition, cool breezes and fogs roll up the rivers, a factor that has enabled Cono Sur to successfully tame Pinot Noir at Chimbarongo.

As yet, there is no defined Rapel style of wine; and apart from Cachapoal Merlot, it is difficult to pin down any grape-region association. Rapel needs time for the jumble of activity to settle down, and allow some sort of pattern to emerge.

Curico Valley

Although only listed as a separate wine region as recently as 1996, the Curico Valley was the first to witness the dawn of the modern era in Chilean winemaking. In 1978 Miguel Torres drove 195 kilometres south from Santiago and bought the small Maquehua bodega. Soon after, he sent out orders for stainless steel, cooling equipment and imported oak barrels in an effort to convert Chilean fruit into world-beating wines. The irony is that the man who nudged his neighbours into action has now been left behind as investment and new ideas have swept through Curico. Today, the wines of Montes, Caliterra, San Pedro and Valdivieso are leading the Chilean charge in export markets. The last two, based in Molina and Lontue respectively, have invested heavily on vineyard expansion and new technology; and have both benefited enormously from the input of foreign consultants.

The Curico region is subdivided into the Teno and Lontue valleys, with a large proportion of vineyards located at Sagrada Familia, where the two rivers meet. Although average summer temperatures vary little from Rapel and Maipo, the important difference is the greater contrast between day and night-time

temperatures, with summer fluctuations of up to 18°C. The slower maturation caused by night-time summer temperatures as low as 5°C, provides ideal conditions for white wines. The Chardonnays and Sauvignons from Curico have joined the wines of Casablanca at the forefront of the Chilean white wine revolution. In the western edge of the region, there are large tracts of unirrigated vines, producing low yields but extremely high quality fruit. Some of the best Cabernet Sauvignon and Merlot fruit in Chile is sourced here, and Valdivieso, in particular has raised the level of its premium reds by maintaining the use of these vineyards.

Maule Valley

Although the largest of Chile's wine producing regions, the Maule valley is the least developed. It is predominantly a white wine region, that although over-bloated with the inferior Pais grape, is being tipped as the place to find Chile's second Casablanca. Top of the list is Cauquenes, close to the coastal range, and whose climate has already been likened to northern Sonoma. Research in this area by the Government-funded Fundacion Chile, has drawn the attention of California giant Kendall-Jackson and the Pernod Ricard group. So far, Chardonnay, Cabernet Sauvignon, Merlot and Sauvignon Blanc have been planted. Apart from Cauquenes which is part of the westerly Tutuven appellation, the main focus of winemaking activity centres on the Claro valley and Loncomilla. Soils are more volcanic than the northerly regions, and around Talca and the Melozal Valley, clay outcrops produce quality Merlot.

Southern Region

This is the great unknown of Chilean viticulture, including the Itata and Bio Bio Valleys. Some of the earliest Spanish vineyards were in the Itata Valley and the tradition has been continued by Fundacion Chile with nearly 200 hectares of experimental Chardonnay, Cabernet Sauvignon, Merlot, Syrah and Cabernet Franc. Further south, plantings of Gewürztraminer and Riesling near Mulchen have brought promising results for Concha y Toro, although frost risk is higher than in Casablanca.

△ *Microclimates vary widely in the Rapel Valley, and encourage experimentation with grape varieties.*

Argentina

It is easy to fall in love with Argentina, a country where the night life begins at 2am, tango is a national obsession and the steaks are as thick as building bricks – if a good deal more edible. Buenos Aires, its capital city, is one of the smartest places in South America, combining Italian chic, Spanish passion and Parisian prices in one characterful package.

Argentina's wines are often a good deal less exciting. With more than 200,000 hectares under vine, Argentina is the fifth largest producer in the world. But we're talking slumbering leviathan here. Until recently, wines from Mendoza or Salta were rarely seen outside Argentina. Argentine drinkers were enthusiastic consumers of the local plonk; and the rest of us were happy to leave them to it.

By international standards, most of the wines were extremely old-fashioned: dried out reds and flabby, fruitless whites. To a certain extent, this is still true. But a new generation of Argentine producers has emerged in the last decade, working alongside foreign winemakers from Australia, France and the US to make fresher, more vibrant wines. Wineries like Catena, Etchart, Norton and La Agrícola are in the vanguard, but their success is beginning to have an effect on the more rustic operations, too.

As well as being the largest wine-producing country in South America, Argentina is also one of the oldest. Its first vines were planted by Jesuit missionaries in the foothills of the Andes in the mid-16th century (a descendant of which still survives in the form of Criolla, the country's staple grape), but it was the completion of the railway line between Mendoza and Buenos Aires in 1885 and successive waves of Italian, French and Spanish immigrants at the turn of the century which created the modern Argentine wine industry.

With further investment in new-fangled, stainless steel technology and lower yields in the vineyard, Argentina could take on the rest of the New World. It has a hot

and generally reliable climate and a line-up of grapes which reflects its people's European origins. Where else can you find Spain's Macabeo, Tempranillo and Garnacha alongside Italy's Sangiovese, Barbera, Dolcetto and Nebbiolo and France's Chardonnay, Malbec and Cabernet Sauvignon? In a world which prizes diversity, Argentina is poised to be a very big player indeed.

The majority of Argentina's vineyards are tucked against the country's western flank, running for over 2,000 kilometres from Salta in the north to Mendoza in the centre and Río Negro to the southeast. For their everyday viticultural backdrop, winemakers are blessed with the spectacular, brooding peaks of the Andes mountains, one of the few things they share with their Chilean counterparts. As the condor flies, the vineyards of Argentina and neighbouring Chile are no more than an hour or two apart, but there are important differences in climate, soils and especially grape varieties between the two.

Mendoza and San Juan

Mendoza is the hub of the Argentine wine industry, a bright, modern city surrounded by wineries and vineyards. The province of the same name contains roughly two-thirds of Argentina's vines (at 250,000 hectares, plantings were even more substantial at their peak in the mid-1970s) and is recognised as the best grape-growing region in the country.

It is no accident that nearly all the major wineries are based here. Mendoza's continental climate is ideal for vinifera varieties, with plenty, but not too much, sun in the summer and early autumn, and low humidity. Clear, unpolluted skies make this a haven for astronomers. The main drawback as far as winemakers are concerned is lack of rainfall, but the Andes are a plentiful source of water for irrigation. This is just as well, as without it the landscape would revert to a state of arid, semi-desert. Summer hail is an occasional risk and the most forward-thinking producers use nets to protect their vines.

The soil types in Mendoza are a mixture of light and sandy and heavier clay-based alluvial soils. Vineyard altitude varies between 500 and 1,200 metres above sea level, depending on proximity to the Andes. The best areas for red wines are Luján de Cuyo, which was awarded its own appellation in 1993, and Maipú. For aromatic whites, higher Andean vineyards, such as the new plantings at Tupungato and Agrelo, are promising. The sandy flatlands to the east of Mendoza are a basic, table wine area suited to heavy crops, as is the sub-region of San Rafael, three hours' drive to the south of Mendoza.

Mendoza's grape-mix is typical of Argentina as a whole, comprising a vast array of the familiar and not so familiar. The predominant grapes are the basic Criolla Grande, Criolla Chica and Cereza, described by one winemaker as 'little pink plums'. Most of these end up in local wines, which is just as well, although I must confess to a fondness for something called Pont l'Evêque.

Much better wines are made from Malbec (especially in Luján de Cuyo), the juicy, Italianate Bonarda, Sangiovese, Merlot and Cabernet Sauvignon for reds and Chardonnay, Chenin Blanc, Sauvignon Blanc and Torrontès for whites. As in Chile,

△ Above left: Rainfall is scarce in the Mendoza Valley so the ice melt water from the Andes is essential for vine cultivation.
Above: Quality grapes for French-supervised production of sparkling wine at Bodegas Chandon, Mendoza.

most of Argentina vineyards are phylloxera-free, so vines are generally ungrafted.

There have been wholesale changes in the vineyards of Mendoza over the last decade, switching from basic grapes to more recognised international varieties. These have been matched by equally important changes in the best, cutting-edge wineries and the introduction of barrel-fermentation for the top Chardonnays and barrel-ageing for a handful of Cabernet and Malbec-based reds.

To the north of Mendoza, San Juan is the second largest wine-producing area in the country, with roughly 25 per cent of Argentina's plantings. The climate is hotter than in Mendoza; the rainfall even lower. Historically, this has been a source of grape concentrate and brandy base wine. In recent years, the area under vine has fallen significantly. Little of the wine made here finds its way onto export markets.

La Rioja, Catamarca, Salta and Jujuy

The northern region is relatively unimportant in terms of quantity (around four per cent of Argentina's vineyards are planted in the four provinces of La Rioja, Salta, Catamarca and Jujuy), but specialises in Argentina's most interesting white grape, the spicy, aromatic, full-flavoured Torrontès. The province of Salta, which contains some cool microclimates as high as 1,500 metres above sea level, is the source of the best Torrontès in the country and some good Cabernet Sauvignon, both of which are distinguished by refreshing natural acidity.

Patagonian region – Neuquén and Rio Negro

The coolest wine-growing region of Argentina is Patagonia, an area better-known for apple orchards and travel writing than for Chardonnay or Sauvignon Blanc. There is undoubtedly potential to make good white wines here, thanks to a combination of a long, slow ripening season, chalky soils and low rainfall. But lack of investment has held the region back. Many believe that Río Negro and Neuquén will emerge as some of Argentina's best areas over the next decade.

The rest of South America

Winemaking is a fairly unsophisticated affair elsewhere in South America, although vines are grown in Venezuela, Peru, Brazil, Colombia, Bolivia and Uruguay. Most of these countries have viticultural roots dating back to the arrival of the Spanish and Portuguese in the 16th century. Despite this pedigree, of the continent's half dozen lesser producers, only Uruguay and Brazil produce consumer-friendly styles in any quantity. Elsewhere grapes are generally used for spirits, such as brandy or pisco.

One notable exception is Peru's Viña Tacama winery, situated at Ica in the foothills of the Andes, which has produced drinkable reds and whites, based on Malbec, Cabernet Sauvignon, Sauvignon Blanc, Chenin Blanc and Colombard for more than 20 years, first with the help of French oenologist, Emile Peynaud, and more recently of Australian winemaker, John Worontschak.

Brazil

Brazil's wine industry is concentrated in the southern tip of the country, close to the border with Uruguay, in Rio Grande do Sul. Initially, it was Italian immigrants who brought vinifera vines to the region, planting grapes such as Bonarda, Barbera, Trebbiano and Moscato in the late 19th century. More recently, multinational companies, such as Martini, Moët & Chandon, and the vast Aurora cooperative, have developed vineyards based on a mixture of Italian and French varieties, including Cabernet Sauvignon, Malbec, Zinfandel, Barbera, Chardonnay, Pinot Blanc and Sémillon, and have introduced modern vinification techniques.

Problems remain, however: hybrid grapes, especially Isabella, still predominate and, in the vineyards, a combination of humidity and high rainfall makes grape growing difficult. As the home market expands, experimental plantings are being made in new areas including the Frontera region next to Argentina and Uruguay, and the Sierra Gaucha hills, where Italian-style sparkling wine is produced.

Uruguay

Uruguay does not make as much wine as Brazil, but the quality of its wines is generally good. Growing conditions in most areas are less humid than in Brazil and the top Uruguayan wines can be a match for all but the best of Chile and Argentina. Viticultural know-how is also comparatively advanced, thanks to the work of the French oenologists, Denis Boubals and Alain Carbonneau, and the Australian Richard Smart.

Uruguay's vineyards are divided geographically into five main regions: the South (Montevideo, Canelones, San José and Florida), the Southwest (Colonia), the Centre (Durazno), the Northwest (Paysandú, Salto and Artigas) and the North (Rivera-Tacuarembo). Of these, the oldest and by far the largest region is the Southern Area, situated 50 kilometres to the south of the capital, Montevideo. (It was here that Spanish and Italian immigrants established the first commercial vineyards.) But small, yet increasingly important, vineyards have been developed in other parts of the country over the last 20 years, especially in Rivera, Colonia and Durazno.

South America's fourth largest wine producing country has a well-established group of wineries, some of which were founded as long ago as the 1870s. The leading names are Castel Pujol, Irurtia, Castillo Viejo and Juanico, all of whom make good wines from grapes such as Cabernet Sauvignon, Merlot, Chardonnay, Sauvignon Blanc, Riesling and Gewürztraminer. Uruguay's most individual variety, however, is the thick-skinned Tannat of southwest France, one of the first vinifera vines to be planted in Uruguay and, many believe, its future star. Plantings are considerable (over 30 per cent of Uruguay's 9,500 hectares) and with the arrival of new, disease-resistant clones, Uruguayan Tannat could well begin to establish itself on the international scene.

Recommended Producers

Chile

Aconcagua Valley

Errázuriz – Alone in the valley, this state-of-the-art winery makes consistently good Cabernet Sauvignon from the Don Maximiano estate. Stylistic fluctuations in recent years have been caused by a lack of continuity in the winemaking department. It makes excellent Chardonnay from Casablanca, and Merlot from Maule valley.

Casablanca Valley

Viña Casablanca – Ignacio Recabarren's creative playpen and the most progressive winery in Casablanca. Excellent Sauvignon Blanc, Chardonnay, and Gewürztraminer come from the Santa Isabel estate. Tiny quantities of impressive low yield Cabernet Sauvignon and Merlot are produced.

Villard Fine Wines – This collaboration between three Chilean growers and Frenchman Thierry Villard, produces Sauvignon Blanc and Chardonnay. The latter shows big vintage variation due to Villard's constant experimentation with different types of oak barrel.

Franciscan – Large estate in the eastern (and warmest) corner of the valley owned by Agustin Huuneus. First releases of Sauvignon Blanc and Chardonnay appeared in 1997. Today the ex-Concha y Toro winemaker Gaetane Carron is in charge of filling up the stainless steel tanks.

Maipo Valley

Aquitania – This estate comprises 25 hectares of Cabernet Sauvignon and Merlot owned by Bruno Prats and Paul Pontallier, blended and bottled under the label Domaine Paul Bruno. The first two vintages were disappointing but 1995 shows much more class. The future depends on the effects of increasing smog and real estate.

Canepa – Workhorse of the supermarket own-label market, but now building the Canepa name with top quality Maipo Cabernet Sauvignon.

Carmen – This hi-tech sister winery to Santa Rita has talented Alvaro Espinosa at the helm. Reds out-perform the whites, particularly the oak aged Merlot Reserve and Gold Reserve Cabernet Sauvignon. Experimental plots of organic viticulture and Italian varietals make this a name to watch.

Concha y Toro – Chile's largest producer with a radical planting programme providing varietals from every region. Top range Casillero del Diablo and Marques de Casa Concha Cabernet Sauvignon showcase Maipo's best fruit, while the new Trio Chardonnay and Merlot give hints of even better things to come. Look out for the recently-released Zinfandel.

Portal del Alto – One of the quiet achievers in the Maipo, producing fine unoaked Cabernet Sauvignon, citrusy Chardonnay, and simple fruit-first Merlot.

Santa Carolina – Because of its ability to dazzle and disappoint in equal amounts, this is one of the more frustrating names in the region. Good Merlot from San Fernando and Cabernet Sauvignon from Maipo have been topped by the arrival of a stunning Malbec. Its Gran Reserva Chardonnay has improved enormously.

Santa Ines – Small, family-run estate in the Isla del Maipo, and one of the few to offer the ancient varietal, Carmenere. A dense, rich Malbec, well-balanced Merlot Reserve, and crisp, unoaked Sauvignon Blanc are the best of the portfolio.

Santa Rita – Old timer on the road to recovery after years of stagnancy. It has a tendency to over-oak the premium reds, but better balance to be found in the 120 range. The new Casablanca Merlot is superb.

Undurraga – Dozing quietly for years, Undurraga has suddenly woken up and decided to replace the once-ubiquitous prefix 'dull' with 'fresh'. The award-winning Chardonnay Reserve 1995 was the first signal, but improving Merlot and Cabernet Sauvignon will keep up the momentum.

William Fèvre Chile – The Burgundian's dream of making great Chilean Chardonnay has focused on vineyards high up in the Cajon del Maipo. The new winery should bring a leap in quality.

Rapel Valley

Casa Lapostolle – The French Marnier-Lapostolle family injected the cash, consultant Michel Rolland supplied the creativity, and the results so far have been impressive. Elegant but steely Sauvignon Blanc; ripe, thick-coated Chardonnay; and the blockbusting Cuvée Alexandre Merlot.

Cono Sur – Dynamic winery whose Chimbarongo Pinot Noir put both the region and the grape on the Chilean map. Cono Sur's portfolio has expanded to four different Pinot versions including a terrific Casablanca model. Tocornal and Isla Negra are the second labels which are offering brilliant value for money.

Luis Felipe Edwards – Grape-grower turned wine producer with huge single estate in Colchagua valley. Chardonnay and Cabernet Sauvignon are made in oaked and unoaked versions, and although early vintages have been rather formulaic, the potential is there.

Santa Emiliana – Consistently good range of varietals under the Andes Peak label (the soft, minty Merlot is particularly good).

Santa Monica – Traditional family-run operation with one of the best (and only) Rieslings in Chile. The Sémillon and Chardonnay have improved dramatically.

Viña La Rosa – This ex-wine supplier to Santa Rita is now the leading winery in the Rapel renaissance. With the help of consultant Ignacio Recabarren, the La Palma range brilliantly showcases the quality of Cachapoal fruit, in particular, the Chardonnay and Merlot.

Viña Porta – Consistently one of the top flight boutique wineries, with a reputation forged on small quantities of rich, finely-textured Chardonnay and Cabernet Sauvignon.

Curico Valley

Caliterra – Joint venture between Errazuriz and Mondavi producing one of the best Chardonnays from Casablanca; impressive Cabernet Sauvignon Reserva from Maipo; and pungent, silky Curico Merlot.

Echeverria – Family-run winery delivering reliable rather than ground-breaking wines. Oak-aged Chardonnay and Cabernet Sauvignon both boast good depth of fruit.

La Fortuna – Great vineyards, shame about the dilapidated winery. Investment required but excellent Malbec and Merlot show the raw materials are there.

Montes – Enough glimpses of brilliance among the patches of mediocrity make this worth watching. Crisp, grassy Sauvignon Blanc is the best of the whites; powerful Malbec, juicily uncomplicated Merlot, and La Finca Cabernet Sauvignon head the reds.

San Pedro – Midway through a period of rejuvenation, and French consultant Jacques Lurton has already raised standards enormously. The improved Gato Negro range offers great value; and up a notch, the Castillo de Molina Cabernet Sauvignon reveals the extent of premium ambitions.

Valdivieso – Chile's largest sparkling wine producer has made massive recent strides with its 'still' portfolio, aided by consultant Paul Hobbs. Extensive tracts of unirrigated vineyards are providing high quality Merlot, Chardonnay and Cabernet fruit. Best known for its classy Pinot Noir Reserve, but even this could be nudged out by the new premium red blend, Cavallo Loco.

Maule Valley

Carta Vieja – Until now, this Talca-based winery has been a sleeping giant, but the move from bulk to bottled wine is revealing some fantastic fruit, particularly its Merlot off the clay-rich soils in the area. Antigua Selection Cabernet Sauvignon has concentration and complexity.

Domaine Oriental – Born of a French-Pacific partnership. The Clos Centenaire range is promising, with a weighty, damson-filled Merlot gaining most points.

Terra Noble – Small, modern outfit still in its infancy, with Loire wizard Henri Marionnet flying in regularly to orchestrate the winemaking. The fragrant Sauvignon Blanc is one of the best from the area; the Merlot is made in the juicy, early-drinking style.

Argentina
Central region

Balbi Small – Old-fashioned winery based in San Rafael, which has benefited from substantial investment by parent company, Allied Domecq, since 1993. The range includes fruity, inexpensive Chenin Blanc, Malbec and Bonarda.

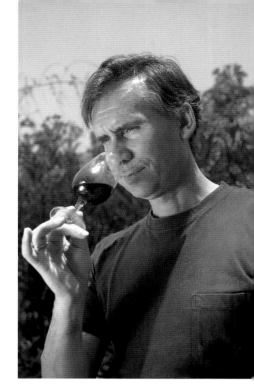

 151

RECOMMENDED PRODUCERS

△ *Ignacio Recabarren, dynamic visionary behind the development of Chile's Casablanca Valley, and winemaker at Viña Casablanca.*

Nicolás Catena – A large, innovative, quality minded group, which owns three principal wineries (La Rural, Escorihuela and Esmeralda) and bottles wines under a number of different labels. International-style Chardonnay, Malbec and Cabernet Sauvignon (Catena and Alamos Ridge) are among the best wines in Argentina, but also good for commercial, cleanly-made reds and whites (La Rural).

Hermanos Lurton – A joint-venture based at the Escorihuela winery between Nicolás Catena and French flying winemaker Jacques Lurton producing fresh, modern, unoaked styles, mainly for the Argentine market. Particularly good for aromatic Chenin Blanc.

La Agrícola – Ultra-modern Mendoza operation with large vineyard holdings, making fruity, well-crafted wines from native as well as international grapes. Labels include Viejo Surco, Picajuan Peak, La Agrícola and Santa Julia. Interesting Bonarda and Sangiovese wines.

Luigi Bosca – Organically-minded, family-owned producer based in the delimited Luján de Cuyo district of Mendoza. Look out for ambitious, if slightly pricey, barrel-fermented Chardonnay as well as full-flavoured Malbec and Syrah.

Navarro Correas – Quality-conscious still and sparkling wine company (the latter made with the help of French Champagne house, Deutz) with vineyards in Maipú, Luján de Cuyo and Tupungato. Rich Chardonnay and a fine, Bordeaux blend-style red, Private Collection.

Nieto y Senetiner – Promising, Luján de Cuyo-based winery, producing rich, deeply coloured reds (the Syrah and Malbec are especially good) and a decent, partially oaked Chardonnay, all under the Valle de Vistalba label.

Norton – Once English, now Austrian-owned, showpiece Mendoza bodega, which has benefited considerably from investment in the winery and the vineyard since 1989. Good Torrontès and very good to outstanding, unoaked red wines from Malbec, Merlot and Cabernet Sauvignon.

Peñaflor/Trapiche – Under-performing giant, divided (in theory) between Peñaflor for everyday drinking and Trapiche for finer wines. The simple Peñaflor bottlings, especially the Tempranillo and Malbec, are often a better bet than those under the Trapiche label, although the arrival of French consultant Michel Rolland appears to have altered the balance of power at this company since 1996.

Weinert – Classic Mendoza winery, now partially owned by Nicolás Catena. Considered by some to among be Argentina's best reds, Weinert's cask-aged Malbecs and Cabernet Sauvignons are well-made, if slightly old-fashioned in style.

Northern region

Etchart – Respected, medium-sized winery owned by the French Pernod-Ricard group. Large vineyard holdings in Cafayate (Salta), the source of Argentina's best Torrontès. Reliable to impressive Cabernet Sauvignon from Mendoza and Cafayate. Avoid the cheaper wines.

△ *Gaetane Carron, winemaker at Franciscan's Veramonte Estate in the Casablanca Valley.*

Index

Figures in bold refer to illustrations

Picture Acknowledgements

Front and back jacket: **Root Stock/Hendrik Holler**

Corbis UK Ltd /Gunter Marx 128 /129, **/Charles O'Rear** 121

Patrick Eagar 50

Root Stock/Hendrik Holler: 5, 6/7,8/9, 10/11, 12/13, 14, 15, 16, 17, 18, 19, 20/21, 22/25, 23 centre left, 23 right, 24, 26/27, 29 , 30/31, 32, 34/35,36/37, 38/39, 40, 42/43, 44/45, 46, 48/49, 52/53, 55, 57, 58, 61, 62/63, 64/65, 68, 69, 71, 73, 74 /75, 77, 78/79, 80/81, 83, 84/85, 86/7, 88/89, 90, 92/93, 95, 97, 98/99, 101, 102/103, 104, 106, 107, 108/9, 111, 112/113, 114/115, 116, 122/123, 124/125, 131, 135, 136/137, 139, 140/141, 142/143, 144/145, 146, 147, 155, 156, **/Montana** 66/67, **/Simi Winery** 133

Jacques Lurton 23 left

John Rizzo 118,119

Scope /Sara Matthews 127

Barry Skipsey 52 left

Richard Smart 23 centre right